Crossing Unmarked Snow

POETS ON POETRY

David Lehman, General Editor
Donald Hall, Founding Editor

New titles

Josephine Jacobsen, *The Instant of Knowing*
Charles Simic, *Orphan Factory*
William Stafford, *Crossing Unmarked Snow*
May Swenson, *Made with Words*

Recently published

A. R. Ammons, *Set in Motion*
Douglas Crase, *AMERIFIL.TXT*
Suzanne Gardinier, *A World That Will Hold All the People*
Allen Grossman, *The Long Schoolroom*
Jonathan Holden, *Guns and Boyhood in America*
Andrew Hudgins, *The Glass Anvil*
Kenneth Koch, *The Art of Poetry*
Martin Lammon (editor), *Written in Water, Written in Stone*
Carol Muske, *Women and Poetry*

Also available are collections by

Robert Bly, Philip Booth, Marianne Boruch, Hayden Carruth,
Fred Chappell, Amy Clampitt, Tom Clark, Robert Creeley,
Donald Davie, Peter Davison, Tess Gallagher, Thom Gunn,
John Haines, Donald Hall, Joy Harjo, Robert Hayden,
Daniel Hoffman, Weldon Kees, Galway Kinnell, Mary Kinzie,
Richard Kostelanetz, Maxine Kumin, David Lehman,
Philip Levine, John Logan, William Matthews, William Meredith,
Jane Miller, John Frederick Nims, Gregory Orr, Alicia Ostriker,
Marge Piercy, Anne Sexton, Charles Simic, Louis Simpson,
William Stafford, Richard Tillinghast, Diane Wakoski,
Alan Williamson, Charles Wright, and James Wright

William Stafford

Crossing Unmarked Snow

FURTHER VIEWS ON THE WRITER'S VOCATION

Edited by Paul Merchant and Vincent Wixon

Ann Arbor

THE UNIVERSITY OF MICHIGAN PRESS

2001   2000   1999   1998   4   3   2   1

A CIP catalog record for this book is available from the British Library.

Library of Congress Cataloging-in-Publication Data

Stafford, William, 1914–
    Crossing unmarked snow : further views on the writer's vocation /
William Stafford ; edited by Paul Merchant and Vincent Wixon.
        p.   cm.
    ISBN 0-472-09664-8 (alk. paper). — ISBN 0-472-06664-1 (pbk. :
alk. paper)
    1. Stafford, William, 1914–   —Authorship.   2. Poetry—History
and criticism.   3. Poetry—Study and teaching.   4. Poetry—
Authorship.   5. Poetics.   I. Merchant, Paul.   II. Wixon, Vincent.
III. Title.
PS3537.T143Z463   1997
811'.54—dc21   97-35257
                                                                 CIP

Acknowledgments: Vincent Wixon gratefully acknowledges the support of
a National Endowment for the Humanities teacher-scholar sabbatical
grant, and of Central Point Schools, Oregon. Paul Merchant is grateful
for financial support from the William Stafford Archive while working
on this volume. Both editors were greatly encouraged in their endeav-
ors by the generosity of the Stafford family. None of this work would
have been possible without the wisdom and expertise of Kim Stafford,
and of his assistant at the Stafford Archive, Diane McDevitt.

Epigraph: From *A Glass Face in the Rain* (New York: Harper and Row,
1982).

Tuned In Late One Night

Listen—this is a faint station
left alive in the vast universe.
I was left here to tell you a message
designed for your instruction or comfort,
but now that my world is gone I crave
expression pure as all the space
around me: I want to tell what is. . . .

Remember?—we learned that still-face way,
to wait in election or meeting and then
to choose the side that wins, a leader
that lasted, a president that stayed in?
But some of us knew even then it was better
to lose if that was the way our chosen
side came out, in truth, at the end.

It's like this, truth is: it's looking out while everything
happens; being in a place of your own,
between your ears; and any person
you face will get the full encounter
of your self. When you hear any news
you ought to register delight or pain
depending on where you really live.

Now I am fading, with this ambition:
to read with my brights full on,
to write on a clear glass typewriter,
to listen with sympathy,
to speak like a child.

—William Stafford

Preface

William Stafford opened ways for others to write by reminding us how deep experience can be, and how accessible. In his own practice, he rose early each morning and drew up net after net filled with the largesse that in fifty years filled thousands of pages in his journal and more than sixty books. Yet when asked which of his poems was his favorite, he replied, "I would exchange all I have written for the next thing." And once in a workshop he said, "I don't want to write *good* poems; I want to write *inevitable* poems—given who I am and what I know, they will come directly from their beginnings." This collection of Stafford's prose pieces, interviews, and poems shows that directness, following in the steps of Stafford's previous books in Michigan's Poets on Poetry series, *Writing the Australian Crawl* (1978) and *You Must Revise Your Life* (1986).

The pieces gathered here show three perspectives on the writer's life. The first suggests how poems can grow—from the immediate moment, or from a journal entry, or even from a simple list of connected ideas. The second is his illuminating readings of other poets' work, and of his own, testing for their validity of experience. The third section describes Stafford's teaching practice, an approach where sage advice on matters of craft is always accompanied by a larger sense of the writer's vocation—as a companion to other seekers in the world, and as witness to each life's moral challenges.

In his own journey, quietly, but with profound authority, Stafford made his stand as a pacifist, as an environmental advocate, and as a westerner, beginning in times when these were lonely positions. Without raising his voice, but trusting his morning discoveries, he used writing to explore his own conscience, and to challenge ours, one poem at a time, setting out over unmarked snow.

                    Paul Merchant and Vincent Wixon

Contents

I
Making Poems

Statements and Poems

All events and experiences are local, somewhere. And all human enhancements of events and experiences—which is to say, all the arts—are regional in the sense that they derive from immediate relation to felt life.

It is this immediacy that distinguishes art. And paradoxically the more local the *self* that art has, the more all people can share it; for that vivid encounter with the stuff of the world is our common ground.

Artists, knowing this mutual enrichment that extends everywhere, can act, and praise, and criticize, as insiders:—the means of their art is the life of their people. And that life grows and improves by being shared. Hence, it is good to welcome any region you live in or come to or think of, for that is where life happens to be—right where you are.

A poem knows where you already are, and it nails you there.

Somewhere deep where we have no program—our next discovery lies.

Last night, sleeping on the floor of the Episcopal Church at Valdez, I dreamed that some old, exposed roll of film had turned up. I held it, ready to develop it, and thought of the scenes, the people, ready there to be mine again, from the vivid, precious past. Without knowing just what they would be I yet hungered for them all.

Writing is like that, I realize: to hold the pen and wait, then start, is like holding that roll of film. Something will come; it will bring from the past. I wait deliciously. And the thing that occurs depends partly on how much I hunger!

≈

For a real writer there are three main ways: morning, afternoon, night.

≈

Always do your writing in the wilderness.

≈

Sermon

Each poem is a miracle that has been invited to happen. But these words, after they come, you look at what's there. Why these? Why not some calculated careful contenders? Because these chosen ones must survive as they were made, by the reckless impulse of a fallible but susceptible person. I must be willingly fallible in order to deserve a place in the realm where miracles happen.

≈

Gold

Mostly it doesn't come knocking at your door—
you have to go looking for it. And it hides among
other rocks, back in canyons. The easy places
have all been cleaned out too. Whole areas
don't have any at all, though various fake pieces
try to act the part. You can tell when you
have it—a soft, easy metal, infinitely adaptable.
If you want it thin, just hammer and it spreads,
but never letting go.

≈

Why I Am a Poet

My father's gravestone said, "I knew it was time."
Our house was alive. It moved,
it had a song. The singers back home
all stood in rows along the railroad line.

When the wind came along the track
every neighbor sang. In the last
house I followed the wind—it
left the world and went on.

We knew, the wind and I, that space
ahead of us, the world like an empty room.
I looked back where the sky came down.
Some days no train would come.

Some birds didn't have a song.

A Slant Message

Tell them how tame geese lure wild ones
close, and then what happens. Go ahead,
explain. Give all the usual reasons
that people use for their treachery.

*Far off, mingled with wind and rain, coasting
their strong wings clearly down a long
staircase of air, the wild ones turn arcs
of trust, mated for life by their truth.*

Sometimes I wake, my wings are set, dawn
has targeted my face, I hear voices
calling me in. My steep dive true
into the world ends my wide dream.

*Faint all day in the sky, trails thrill
their way, like this, into my talk, my telling.*

The things you do not have to say make you rich. Saying things you do not have to say weakens your talk. Hearing things you do not need to hear dulls your hearing. And things you know before you hear them—those are you, those are why you are in the world.

❧

Language can do what it can't say.

❧

No matter who claims them, all good poems, the kind that are organically grown, are anonymous. They come from a saved-up need that the language feels; and you or I can come along, touching into life again the vigor in talk that sleeps in the terms and pauses and constructions residual from earlier encounters with experience in its ups and downs and quirks. Sometimes a path opens in language; you follow it as it goes, like a plan. It guides you where you wanted to go, but didn't know you wanted to till it happens. You can't say you intended it, or even found it, but you are glad you are where you are. It was just a path that opened; you used it. Now you look back and admire. Masterly! You have found a poem.

❧

Some poems link so closely to the writer's intentions or need that they should remain unchanged—not a good poem but something else is the main motive behind the creating of it.

❧

"It was only recently that I was able to write this poem." Often I hear this statement or its equivalent, which implies that writing is something other than just an intention and the craft to carry out the intention.

❧

Prose we can paraphrase; our experiences we can repeat; our knowledge we can add to by little increments; our educations we can sort of *rototill.* We go through routines in education all the time. But sometimes we hunger to do something once-for-all, in immediate quality—we want *art*. And we want not discursive words, but *poetry*. We'll stop and make experience stand and deliver, as the old highwaymen used to say.

It is this impulse to change the *quality* of experience that I recognize as central to creation. Something did not exist—you make it. You are utterly responsible: out of all that could be done, you choose one thing. What that one thing is, nothing else can tell you—you come at it over unmarked snow. This experience of freedom becomes your addiction: you rarify and rarify it. The thing you make is nothing but itself; between you and it there is an inviolable congeniality; but to others what you make may appear some kind of irresponsible affront. You are not persuading someone in politics; you are not selling some product; you are not winning friends; you are not writing in order to get into print in any magazine. What, then, are you doing? You and your materials are responsive to each other to the exclusion of all else.

Poetry

Its door opens near. It's a shrine
by the road, it's a flower in the parking lot
of The Pentagon, it says, "Look around,
listen. Feel the air." It interrupts
international telephone lines with a tune.
When traffic lines jam, it gets out
and dances on the bridge. If great people
get distracted by fame they forget
this essential kind of breathing
and they die inside their gold shell.
When caravans cross deserts
it is the secret treasure hidden under the jewels.

Sometimes commanders take us over, and they
try to impose their whole universe,
how to succeed by daily calculation:
I can't eat that bread.

Don't have any standards outside the feeling you have as you write. Just follow your impulse, enjoy what happens. Permit yourself to like what you are doing (if you feel any qualms, then veer toward what feels good—why oppose the only compass you have?).

ॐ

The first thing you think of is really worth writing down. And the second. And the third. . . .

ॐ

Writing a poem is not to be considered as "a problem." A poem is a solution for a problem before the problem occurs.

ॐ

A writer must write the bad poems in order to approach the good ones—finicky ways will dry up the sources.

ॐ

Some poems may cry out for revisions; but some—even though perhaps regrettable—are impervious to ready criticism. We may say to these poems, "Be born again."

ॐ

A poem may be indicted for weaknesses, without thereby yielding itself to correction: there may be flaws necessary for even the faltering accomplishment embodied in the poem. To avoid the flaws might make the poem miss its goal even further than it does now.

ॐ

Receiver

Listening late at parties, hearing
the quiet ones, dead keys on the piano
lifting their deep report, how they
used to have names to drop all evening
before those rooms went dark—

Such times I've gone out alone, quiet
in the woods, and waited by a little fire:
that's when the night-room comes, hovering
near, hollowed out by an owl,
and I in the center to hear—

Or out along water, to put in my hand
under the starlight: before the shine,
a little ripple begins, and a fragile
white web floats up, a message for someone
like me, far, there on the shore.

Waiting for Poems to Come

Whenever they come I keep them as still
as I can and let them out one by one.
They fly toward sunset, and I follow them. Or in the dark
late I listen. Their wings guide me, a step
at a time, their flight my walk, their fear mine.

Many of them wander out beyond sunset
and come back changed. You can study them
stopped by the camera and then enlarged
and thought about, disappearing as they
find themselves acknowledged by light.

This is not the sort of thing that critics
monitor, but it makes a difference in your mind
especially toward evening when poems go by.
What will you do with important things in your life
that no one notices? It's a problem for everyone.

These odd creations know a music unknown to me.
They follow a coastline under the clouds. Their cries
come back where I am and I lean after them to reach
as far as I can. Only a faint answer
comes back, and I think: "They have that other world."

Their world waits in my silence. I let the still rain
fall. Far off the poems' almost-presence could be

whispering but they are gone so far the air
won't carry even the echo of what they were.
I wait and in the land they left the still rain falls.

Nothing in the afternoon, only a breeze
that lifts your hair. No sound but
elm leaves, the recurrent lisping of surf.
Maybe no poem will ever come to your island.
Why does a day like this slip into the world?

Some day all our poems will blend together: only
the voice of our years, only a far-off wind.

This way of writing, it's as if I'm setting forth partly holding my breath, partly almost like dancing. The movement is for another purpose, a gathering purpose, a seeking of a feeling while I go. In the air I breathe, a little extra savor comes, a tang of sage or pine. Some surprise, some hint of a great change almost, almost, happens. This elation enhances the present moment; it is partly a result of past bonus experiences and partly a cause for new bonus experiences.

Whispering into my ear, the syllables rustle their plumes and settle beside each other; longer and shorter phrases parade back and forth encouraging and urging forward. Little glimpses, and sometimes huge fleeting panoramas, flicker just outside the main line of my attention.

Throughout this spell, no one else intrudes for long: every move I make, every adjustment, retreat, surge onward, is profoundly individual, all my own, not lonely, just alone, a consciousness that must be aware of its unique reception amid a great, breathless moment of becoming.

Inhabiting a Song

Somewhere back of my throat a tune
hovers. My voice or the ghost of my voice

follows, repeating words and weaving
a record of my life into waves and hesitations.

Suppose our chorus, people and animals,
rises and falls in intervals of breath:
in sleep a dog's paw twitches; a rabbit's
dream follows its heartbeat all the way
through some ballad that its life is.

Parts of my song disappear, fade out
except for a beat that spans a known
part to another known part, and on.
Even in silence when shadows pass
my throat is full of the sound of the world.

"All events and experiences are local . . . ," from *Tennessee Poetry Journal* (Fall 1967); "A poem knows where you already are . . ." and "Always do your writing in the wilderness" from Stephen Kuusisto, Deborah Tall, and David Weiss, eds., *The Poet's Notebook* (New York: Norton, 1995); "Each poem is a miracle . . . ," preface to *An Oregon Message* (New York: Harper and Row, 1987); "Gold," unpublished, July 15, 1993; "Why I Am a Poet," from *My Name Is William Tell* (Lewiston, ID: Confluence Press, 1992); "A Slant Message," from *Wilderness,* January 1993; "No matter who claims them . . . " from "How It Is to Write Poetry Today," unpublished essay, after July 1986; "Prose we can paraphrase . . . " from a reading at Lewis and Clark College, Portland, Oregon, January 30, 1958; "Poetry," from *Even in Quiet Places* (Lewiston, ID: Confluence Press, 1996); "Receiver," from *A Glass Face in the Rain* (New York: Harper and Row, 1982); "Waiting for Poems to Come," unpublished, July 1986; "This way of writing . . . ," unpublished, October 22, 1988; "Inhabiting a Song," unpublished, August 8, 1993. Prose statements, Daily Writings 1958–1991, by permission of Estate of William Stafford; except where noted, all poems by permission of Estate of William Stafford.

The Experience of Now
A Dialogue with Students

This encounter depends on all of us, and my excuse for being here is that, as a matter of fact, I have tried to write almost every day for a lifetime. I'm just in writing. I was going to say, of course, there are a lot of us, but there aren't very many people who are just all-purpose writers. I'll take my stand as an all-purpose writer. I get here as a poet, but I'll write anything you like—an ad, a slogan; if you want a new Bible, it'll take a little longer. Anything. Do you think of some issues we could explore?

What is the potential for motivating people towards change through writing? I'm interested in reform and acting against problems, things like that. What's the actual impact of writing?

I take a breath on this because actually when I said there are a lot of us writers, I think there are a lot of people trying to change others through writing. I don't so much represent that group here, but I like to address what you're saying and I'm interested, of course, in changing people in the right way. But the kind of writing I've done has mostly been a kind that is much less focused or aimed than that. It's more like finding out what you want to write about every morning and then writing about it, whether it happens to fit your national priorities or not. It's poetry or creative writing, but, of course, there are just so many people using language to persuade others that I don't know

Interview, Willamette University, April 13, 1987; portions used in *William Stafford: What the River Says,* TTTD Productions, 1989, videocassette.

what to say about that. Here's the reason I'm dithering about it. All the points of view that people are trying to put forward can be served by language. This kind of encounter here, I was thinking, is one in which we consider not what we're going to do about society or issues and so on, but in what way can the language itself and our relation to it help us do whatever we're going to do. I think there's a lot being done, and a lot can be done with the language to persuade people. But so far as I'm concerned it's sort of self-canceling. You know, there are all those evil people also persuading people. And sometimes I think there are more of them.

So I'm almost sorry that the language can be used that way. And suddenly I realize I've evaded this issue a little in my life by shrugging it off. Thinking, well if I write when it comes to me and if I find my way forward by the experiences I'm having, then maybe what comes to me and what results from my encounter with the language will be new to other people and it somehow will be on the leading edge of what's happening in our time. But I don't know what it is. I mean, it's not aimed. See, I'm floundering. But I think it's an issue I certainly haven't settled before us. What shall we do? How can we stop all those people from writing? I mean the wrong people. See, that's another topic. And it might be more important than learning to write ourselves.

What makes the wrong person the wrong person?

From my point of view—it's easy for me now because all of my experience is backing me up here. I realize that way off somewhere God or someone is saying, "Yeah, yeah, that's what you say"—from my point of view, the people who are wrong are the ones who are using language in order to increase the intensity of the problems rather than solving the problems. They're people who are going to overwhelm their audiences with rhetoric, with partial truths. It's an almost universal tactic in the legislature, in political speeches, in magazine articles.

As an intellectual I speak to you in a university. So let me appeal to you. What we have, the glimmer we have in front of us, is the possibility that if we all key ourselves up enough and are alert enough, and are not satisfied with partial truths, partial information, we may find our way to some kind of betterment. But even most writing courses you take will have to do with how to increase your effectiveness as a writer, not with how to find out what in the world you're trying to do anyway. The aim is so important. And competition, from my point of view, is so unimportant in writing. I'm thinking about all the forensic people who are here to sell us a bill of goods. They're the ones I mean are wrong. In a university we're used to meeting people under conditions where we can talk back and forth and consider and find our mutual way.

I like your poetry. This'll show my ignorance, but why do you write poetry? To communicate, or do you write it for yourself?

I write it for myself mostly. I felt brave when I said that. And you notice I said mostly. Now I want to wiggle a little bit. The main feeling I have when I'm writing is that I'm seeking the satisfactions that are in the arrivals at the moment in language for me. There are little emergent discoveries, opportunities while I write. And those are so satisfying that that's what I do. It's not the money. There could be money maybe, but that can't be the primary thing for the kind of writing I'm talking about. Because its direction and effectiveness depend on your total commitment to letting the experience of now take you to where the main tides of your life and the opportunities of language will take you.

There are ways to write in which you may suppress your own feelings. Suppose you start to write for some cause you believe in and suddenly you're smitten with the recollection or a realization that there's something in that cause or some recent thing that's been done by people in that cause that would spoil your case. So you suppress it. That would be one way. It wouldn't be my way. I feel that the university way, the intellectual way, the way I want to promote here, is to face all the complexities of your thought as you go along. And there's such exhilaration in letting yourself become caught up in what you're creating that you are no longer paying attention to subsidiary things, like the cause. This is why artists get in such trouble. This is why Solzhenitsyn was forced out of the Soviet Union. They're not writing for the audience that's right there to pay them or pet them. They are caught up in a kind of progressive discovery of something. And so you can't trust artists. But I don't want to trust artists. I don't want to trust the people who are trying to suppress the artists. I want to go along for the ride when I'm writing. And it's like downhill skiing. Someone might say, "Well, why do you do it? What's in it for you?" Well, I don't know. It just feels good.

When you say you write for yourself, do you ever write for yourself in order to share yourself with others? Do you ever have that idea in mind? Do you want to write about something that you think about in a way so that someone can see it from your point of view at all?

Maybe I do. It's hard for me to deny that this happens sometimes. But my impulse is to deny that, and then make my life live up to what I'm denying. It's not like sharing yourself with others because that implies that there is something you've already accomplished that you want to give to others. But the kind of writing I'm talking about is like thinking. It is the free dive into the experience of now. So the nowness of experience . . . and if you let yourself do that, it's not a self that you're presenting to others. It's a kind of going along together for what's in the language at this moment to someone from your background. But it's not like having prepared a position that you are now presenting to the world. It's that part that I was trying to deny.

Most people talk about writing as a . . . maybe on the board I can do this. *[Draws two stick figures on blackboard]* Here's the self you were talking about, the writer or the talker. And over here is the reader or the listener. And most people say, "Well I'm going to take myself and somehow I'm going to do something for or to or about this person. I'm going to change them somehow." Most people think of it that way.

I envision it like this. Between us there's language. When I write or talk, I just dive into the language. Even if I start a sentence like this, which I've just started now, without figuring out how in the world I'm going to end it, I know that I'm going to be able to end it, because I've done many sentences sort of like this, and no matter how many parentheses I put in, I find my way out at the end. OK? *[Laughter]*

Now, you see I didn't have time to think about what is somebody else thinking about while I'm saying this. You know it gets impossibly complex. But if I just dive into the language it takes care of me. The language takes care of a writer or a talker.

When you dive into the language you somehow know that you're going to produce response from a person. You have to know that somewhere, or you wouldn't write, would you?

You make it sound as if anything you say or anything you write is for the purpose of persuading or changing. Well, now you have friends and you're talking. You're talking happily. And these friends, while you're talking, you're thinking, "What do I want to do to my friend today? How do I want to change my friend?" You don't really do that. That's a haunted, that's like a nightmare world. Imagine we're surrounded by people who have gone through universities that teach them to do this. Think of your audience. What do you want to accomplish? OK, see your friend today, and operate. No, you don't do that. Instead you meet your friend, you get excited, they say something, you say, "Oh, but wait." And even when you think you're throwing him off, or, you know, turning him off, you can't stop anyway. You just keep driving your point home. Isn't that right? And it's the excitement you have yourself rather than your plot against or for your friend. Isn't that right? That's the kind of world I want to be in. I don't want my friends, having passed all these courses so every time they meet me they think, "Now, OK, I'm going to change Bill a certain way today."

Where's this writing come from? It seems like a lot of people write from their pains, they write from their agonies, they write from their desires, they write from their need for faith. Where would yours originate?

Well, what I'm afraid of is that I'll sound as if anyone who did believe me would think that I must be really odd. But actually in the real world, for instance, you go to a party. And those people there are just whirling around talking, and all sorts of things are happening, and they're happy or they're sad, or whatever. It would take quite a bit of artifice to tie all their activity to their desire to express their pains, or to change the people at the party. I mean, someone goes to a party in order to change the people there—I don't want that kind at my party. Do you? I mean, what goes on all the time, day after day, people do it exactly the way I'm saying. I mean, they talk for the fun of it. They feel satisfactions when they say some things, and a little discouragement when they say other things. And why can't we write that way? Why can't we write for the adventure that there is and what comes to us when we enter a sustained relation to the language?

I didn't invent this language. It's something that came along. I have grandchildren. I listen to them talking to themselves. They're saying little songs or little sayings. They're doing all sorts of things. They don't even think anyone's overhearing them. This kind of activity between you and the language is what makes the great difference between a person who is a writer and a person who has stealthy designs on other people. So it seems to me.

Anyone can have stealthy designs on someone else's ideas. And in our society we seem to feel from the way we teach people and the way we try to help each other, we seem to feel that you can live a life like that, in which there's never any aim except prevailing. I mean you get a job to sell shoes or sell something, and so you try to change people's ideas about it. And they pay you for it. I can understand this. But if they're not paying you for it, or if you happen to know there are some other better kind of shoes somewhere, then it begins to be a strain on your character and your future prospects for the life hereafter if you don't turn honest.

And so I feel trapped in a society, and in a school system, that persuades individuals that all their activities are goal-oriented towards some goal that doesn't have anything to do with how they feel. In the arts it has to do with how you feel. So you trust what occurs to you. And you've just got to do that. If somebody else doesn't like it that way, you can make it the way they like it if you want to, but it won't be art. See what I mean?

The writer goes into the language; the reader or hearer (and this is the writer or speaker) also jumps into the language, I mean from the other side. A miraculous thing happens. Communication takes place. That's what language does. I didn't invent it. I couldn't have invented it. I don't control it. I go along with it. Someone says, "Well, this word used to mean *that* and now it means *this*." I'm not the kind of guy who says, "No, no, it's always *that*." I go along with how the language goes. OK, that's what it means to you. It begins to mean that to me. But that's the genius of the language, not my purpose. So that's part of it.

Maybe we should have a difference here, but, in my own life I write a lot and most of what I write nobody ever sees. Nobody. And even the things I think I've finished, my family doesn't see. I mean the people close to me don't see it. If I think it's something that is like a part of a dialog that's going on in a magazine—the *American Scholar, Atlantic,* I'm not trying for highfalutin things, so I'll say, *Milkweed Chronicle,* you know, any kind of little frivolous magazine—if it seems like something that might be in there, then maybe I send it there after it's written. But I don't write it for that. I write it for that sort of tractoring forward, I'm getting somewhere feeling, umm, good. Tastes good to me. And then if it looks to me as if it might taste good to somebody else, I send it off to an editor. So maybe I'm separating myself from some people here by saying, "Well, I don't write, even for the editor." No, so I'll quote Gandhi to you. A soldier said to Gandhi, "Great One, when shall I lay down my rifle?" And Gandhi said, "When you have to." This is exactly the feeling I would have about what I write. When should you read my poems? It's up to you, you know. If you have to, OK. But I'm not asking you to. Same for the editor. The editor's got to have to.

There's just one other thing I want to say. I want to take a stand for writers. In school you usually are given it like this: find out what an editor wants and then give the editor what the editor wants. Or the teacher, or whatever. No, no, no. Editors can't write their magazines. I mean if an editor knew exactly what the editor wanted they could write it themselves. They don't know. I mean, writers have got to do it. So, suddenly I'm ambitious. What I bring to you folks is a glimpse of the art process, which is not what you've been told it is. It's something that comes right out of your own druthers, your own feelings. Go ahead, go ahead, save me from my sermon.

How can we track that? We're told in college to substantiate our writing. It's usually academic. We're trying to prove something to our teachers that we are right. And yet we cannot be our own authority.

It's very complex here because if you are a rational human being, alert, your teacher doesn't have to tell you you can't be your own authority. You know it yourself, I mean, and if you do know something, then you are the authority. See, there's a little burble here. Let me start with the scene on a campus. Say the teacher is very generous, gives you two or three weeks, and says, do a research paper and write the definitive work on . . . well, one that I saw not too long ago was "The Mistakes of Eisenhower in the Normandy Campaign," written by a high school kid. I imagined Eisenhower reading this! Who's the authority? But anyway, you are given this time to do research. You go to the library and some of the books are out, you don't have that much time, and then you're sort of stupid and you don't understand some of it anyway, so you do whatever you can to lay it on the teacher.

But if you're a writer, now I'm not talking about the kind of writer that's trying to flimflam society. If you're Solzhenitsyn, if you're Tolstoy, if you're these people who are art writers, then the research for what you're writing is your whole life. I mean there is one world expert on it—you. And you're right in the center of your life. So it's not a question of whether you can fool someone else if you're an authority or not. It is that for what you're writing, if you're doing it this way, there is no other authority. There is no other authority. That's where it is. I know I've left a lot of holes here. But it's your fault. All these big questions. We're not going to settle it.

The glimmery I'd like to hold before you is, there is a knack, there is a way of working with the material of your art. In this case it happens to be language. Now I'm doing clay or something. You work with the material of your art and you learn from it. It signals back. You learn from the clay, you learn from the colors. And the difference between the artist and someone who isn't an artist isn't that the artist is smarter or something like that. An artist is doing the art. They're working with the material. So you've got a great bounce ahead of other people. And that doesn't mean that we live in a world where you'll always be rewarded and get publication. That's not true. But to get publication by another means is to take part in the segment of your society that is in this dreadful situation that we're in, you know, processing fakery over and over. And so there'll be some people who will read what you write who will say, "I don't get it." They don't get it. That's all. I mean it takes a certain amount of activity, maybe, on the part of the reader, or a listener. And there are some people who aren't ready for that. Well, maybe they're ready for something else. But they're not ready for—and surely this is proved again and again in the university—they're not ready for Milton. So should Milton somehow be lessened? So he'd get published? That isn't the way he saw it.

Don't you think when someone like Yeats wrote a love poem, he was trying to influence somebody in his writing?

I want to drift back into this. I think that it gave him satisfaction to do poems like that, for instance. He couldn't do it without the satisfaction and have it be art. You see what I'm getting at? I do agree that there are many people who get satisfaction out of using the language in a way to accomplish certain ends. And I can understand that. But you must check it in yourself. And when I was responding I was saying, "Am I thinking about them? No, I'm thinking about me." It must have given Yeats a great charge to say, in "Easter 1916," "a terrible beauty is born," and so on. So yes, satisfaction. His satisfaction. Not his society's satisfaction, not his teacher's satisfaction. But you know, students have to go through this. But there are also teachers who are looking for art. Don't forget that.

What advice could you give somebody who's trying to get some sort of definitive voice, some voice that's constant throughout their work, and can't do it?

One part of me says you're lucky. You can do all kinds of things. So long as you have the impulse to do all those things I say, that's good. That's part of you. And especially maybe that's part of youth. I hope it's part of me too, to be various. Keep on being various. I'm not trying to get myself in a groove. The very spaciousness that you feel may be part of your true voice. So I think the way to do it is not to try, not to choose a voice: one of your voices decides, that's me from now on. But instead to keep on giving your attention where it is solicited most coercively by the impulses you have when you're writing. And that will be you. I mean you will be distinctive because you are different. Everyone's different. So the achievement of a different voice is not an achievement, it's a plight.

Your voice is fastened on you. And you can keep people from knowing what that voice is, but I don't think that you can get a voice that's any good without letting your whole self be that person. So I keep hearing people say you should find a voice and then use it. And they want to be, they want some, Dylan Thomas, or some sonorous voice, whereas maybe their true voice is some kind of whining voice. Well, that's what they ought to do. Then pretty soon they'll become Kafka or someone. And you imagine Kafka says I'm going to be like . . . and then chooses someone he couldn't possibly be like anyway, though he could fake it. But we wouldn't have Kafka.

You said you've written in different forms, but what makes poetry special to you? Why do you write poetry?

Poetry has a different feel to me. Everything makes a difference, and a crucial difference, in poetry. You're tuned up more with poetry. Prose, we're so much in the habit of thinking we can read directions on a bottle, or stop, go or whatever, and we're not really fully alerted. But if someone says something in a way or puts on the page in such a way that you know it's a poem, then you listen or read with a different kind of intensity, it seems to me. So to me poetry is just language that is souped up and ready for the events that are really endemic in any language, but are more frequent in poetry maybe.

You mentioned Yeats earlier. What do you think about the public responsibilities of the poet?

Now I don't know how much time we have, but I came here to give an invocation at the opening of the House session across the street at the capitol. And I have in my pocket what I brought, and this sort of relates to what you're saying. You see, now that church and state are separate or are supposed to be, they can no longer get in there and, you know, say "In Jesus' name," or something like that. I mean it's getting a little bit thick for people who don't say that, or don't believe that. So now they still need dignified language. Society needs dignified language, but they can't use the Bible or the Koran or the Book of Mormon or whatever. So I'll read you what I brought for the Oregon House session, April 13, 1987:

> This hall recalls that one where warriors watched
> a sparrow fly from darkness, traverse their banquet
> table, and disappear into the night:
> that flight symbolized a life, and the warriors
> heard, in Anselm's story, how every person appears
> from the unknown, enjoys light, and goes alone
> away from this world into the dark.
>
> A like sojourn is ours today:
> out in the woods and salal, in the rabbitbrush
> and sage, along the coast, up in the mountains,
> Oregon waits. Days and nights will pass:
> our people will watch and wonder. Secure here
> we can stumble and still govern, trusted: but always
> parts of our state will depend on this hall.
>
> Only the people voted, but the animals too are there,
> and the salmon testing silt in their home rivers.
> Even the trees deserve a place, and the hills
> maintaining their part, while the rocks are quietly
> mentioning integrity.
>
> We start. We cherish this hall, and keep it
> for justice and all good works, and for the world we have
> while we traverse its warmth and light,
> inheritors from those who went before
> and keepers of faith for those who are to come.

Poems on Keeping a Journal

What's in My Journal

Odd things, like a button drawer. Mean
things, fishhooks, barbs in your hand.
But marbles too. A genius for being agreeable.
Junkyard crucifixes, voluptuous
discards. Space for knickknacks, and for
Alaska. Evidence to hang me, or to beatify.
Clues that lead nowhere, that never connected
anyway. Deliberate obfuscation, the kind
that takes genius. Chasms in character.
Loud omissions. Mornings that yawn above
a new grave. Pages you know exist
but you can't find them. Someone's terribly
inevitable life story, maybe mine.

From *Passwords* (New York: HarperPerennial, 1991).

The Way I Write

In the mornings I lie partly propped up
the way Thomas Jefferson did when he slept
at Monticello. Then I stop and
look away like Emily Dickinson when
she was thinking about the carriage and the fly.

When someone disturbs me I come back
like Pascal from those infinite spaces,
but I don't have his great reassurances
of math following along with me; so somehow
the world around me is even scarier.

Besides, the world on fire of Saint Teresa
surrounds me, and the wild faces Dante
awakened on his descent through those dark
forbidden caverns. But over my roof bends
my own kind sky and the mouse-nibble sound of now.

The sky has waited a long time
for this day. Trees have reached out,
the river has scrambled to get where it is.
And here I bring my little mind
to the edge of the ocean and let it think.

My head lolls to one side as thoughts
pour onto the page, important
additions but immediately obsolete, like waves.
The ocean and I have many pebbles
to find and wash off and roll into shape.

"What happens to all these rocks?" "They
become sand." "And then?" My hand stops.
Thomas Jefferson, Emily Dickinson,
Pascal, Dante—they all pause too.
The sky waits. I lean forward and write.

Opening the Moment

A Conversation with Steven Ratiner

Can you set the scene for us: If we were looking in on the start of your work day, what would we see?

My morning writing would begin for me by getting up about four o'clock. Every other morning I take a run, about three miles, and on such mornings as that I would still get to my writing by about five. Then I would have an uninterrupted time until about seven or a little later, at which time my wife would naturally get up. I lie down on the living room couch in front of a big, I guess you would say, picture window which looks out on our quiet neighborhood. The giant fir trees, some other shrubs and trees, rhododendrons and so on outside. I'm lying there relaxed. I have a blank sheet in front of me. I put the date on top, and I start letting whatever swims into my attention get written down on the page. I probably have as relaxed an approach as anybody does. I welcome anything that comes along. I don't have any standards. I know that I'm the only one that is going to see this, unless something eventuates that I think might be helpful to an editor. I put it this way because I am not trying to contend for a place in magazines or in books. I'm just letting my attention flow where it wants to flow. And the relaxation of it is part of the charm for me.

Where do the beginning points come from: from within the room, the imagination?

From *Christian Science Monitor,* August 21, 1991.

I immediately think of really barefoot beginnings of poems. I think of one that starts, "Walls when they meet, hold each other up, the ceiling goes out. . . ." So I mean, I'm looking at the room I'm in. Or it may be the sound of the birds outside, or it might be the residue left from a dream I just left from my sleep. I don't try for being relevant to current experience but if it invites itself, I welcome it. The feeling is of greeting anything at the door and saying, "Come on in."

As both poet and teacher, you've been open and generous about the process that produces your work. What does such extreme receptivity give you as a writer?

For one thing, I think it's a defense against being stampeded by current, intentional engagement with what other people think is important. It's very subjective, but it is the kind of subjectivity that makes you available for what is [making] a valid, actual individual impression on a human being: yourself. I'm afraid that getting published has often pushed me toward trying to repeat what has succeeded, and I don't want to do that. I want to stay as trusting and innocent as I was when I first started to write, and I don't want to have presumptions that what I write will be accepted.

I've read your poetry for many years now, and it seems to me that you are not only willing but take almost a pleasure in allowing yourself to be lost. I was not surprised to see in your new collection, Passwords, *the poem called "The Day Millicent Found the World." Millicent kept pushing further and further into the woods until finally she knew she was "Lost. She had achieved a mysterious world / where any direction would yield only surprise." What is it in "being lost" that holds such allure for you?*

I believe it's kind of an emblem for that deliciousness that I was trying to get into my explanation earlier about the "delicious writing" of the early morning. That if you're lost enough, then the experience of now is your guide to what comes next. None of us knows what comes the next second. We manage to survive in our lives by staying inside the bubble of our assumed self-sufficiency. That's nice, cozy—but as a writer, as a thinker, as maybe a meditator, I have a sense of being in a set of circumstances that's much more wilderness than most people assume.

Much of the time, we are willing to do almost anything rather than face the unknown, the wilderness. When we drive in our cars, we'll go on for endless miles, rather than admit we're lost. We drive our lives that same way until a crisis stops us. But that fear blunts our experience of the world, doesn't it?

Yes. One of the metaphors I have thought of before . . . oh, we had a dog, an Airedale, who would stick his nose out the window when we were driving. And I would see that eager sniffing, inhaling experience the dog was having and I would think: if only I could get the world like that.

How long has this daily regimen been a part of your life?

Well, I became vividly aware of doing it regularly in about 1942.

After five decades of this discipline, can you say how this has shaped your life's experience?

I give a sigh, because I realize that the first thing that occurred to me was that it's made it lonely. I believe it was Clarence Day who [said that] in the novels of Joseph Conrad you get the feeling of [being] on a ship where they're all below celebrating, and there is someone up there at the bow of the boat who realizes how deep the ocean is down there, and where they are going, and that around them is this mystery. So getting up early and being receptive like this, day after day, is a reminder of the depth and mystery around us. I think another thing is: Your life gets centered all over again every day. The daily practice is enough to take you out of the current of your obligations and put you in relation all over again to something that feels like the big current outside of us, the tide of the eventfulness of being alive.

For most of us, it is only the rare moments, of some surprise or emergency, that make us so fully awake, present to our experience. It requires an act of great will.

On the campus where I was teaching, someone said to me about the time I retired, "Well, Bill, you still writing as much as ever?" and my impulse to respond was, "Yes, but I'm trying to taper off." The person who was asking me was thinking, "Oh, this is someone who has to nerve himself to do it," but I turned it around thinking: I'd have to nerve myself *not* to. To some people this seems surprising, even other writers I talk to.

By the way, maybe my circumstances have helped or hurt me into this. Let me explain what I mean. When I said I could remember vividly starting in 1942, that was when I was drafted, right after Pearl Harbor. I was sent off to a conscientious objectors' camp, and in that camp your life was suddenly drastically changed from outside. It was like a work camp or prison camp.

How did that prompt the beginning of this writing method?

Well, it made me want to preserve a part of my life for my own. And the early morning was free time. The government never thought of harnessing us at four in the morning. They thought they were being cruel if they harnessed us at seven-thirty. Well, that gave me three and a half hours of freedom.

I think this has been the situation for many women poets—Sylvia Plath comes to mind—who, because of their commitments as mothers and wives, would get up earlier than their children in order to have time to write.

Yes, in fact, often when I meet people and they talk about not having time to write, I have to avert my eyes, not to look accusingly at them.

But if this pure spontaneity is a proper orientation for writers, what does that say about academia that wants to hand down the traditions and the critical standards?

Well, I think at least on the face of it, it seems there is a conflict here. I don't think that there really is because, in the best kind of education, there is a leading-forth of what is available to the individual human being. It is not so much like putting an overlay, some kind of grid on the developing person. The kind of education I am interested in, the kind of education I think I profited from has been the welcoming process, allying the self to what is available to *that self*... at *that* time. But there are many people who teach in the University who are *professors* of writing, not writers. There are professors of philosophy, not philosophers. Wittgenstein made a big distinction. When I first read him it was like a breath of fresh air, by the way, and I thought: Yes! [There is a way] for forwarding the explorations of the individual soul in this life. That is different from the [tradition] that says: Now I will give you the standards, now I will give you the marks to shoot at. Recently, I read someone's article that said, "You can't be a writer now, if you haven't read ... ," and then he named off a certain bunch of our own peers, you know current fashionable writers. And I thought, "Poor Sophocles!"

The professors I have valued the most have been the kind who would listen in a kind of limber way as conservation was going on, and they would embrace the possibility of confessing to whatever ignorance they felt. Then there is the other way, that is to try to be invulnerable, to put on the armor, to wear your Phi Beta Kappa button and lecture others.

That way props up the "little" self, and probably makes you feel better when you go to bed at night—and it actually impoverishes you.

I feel it does. Armor is fine, but it keeps you from knowing what the weather is like. I feel that one [must] stay flexible, stay a participant.

Clearly the real value for you lies in the process, not simply the final product. But I'm curious about what rests at the heart of this process. There is a line in one of your essays that says, "It is as if the ordinary language we use every day has a hidden set of signals, a kind of secret code." A secret code implies a message from someone or somewhere. What are you tuning into?

I think that what is there in the language is the history of the language. Sort of what Nietzsche was getting at when he said, "Any word with a history can't be defined," or that "every word is a prejudice." I have this feeling of wending my way or blundering through a mysterious jungle of possibilities when I am writing. This jungle has not been explored by previous writers. It never will be explored. It's endlessly varying as we progress through the experience of time. The words that occur to me come out of my relation to the language which is developing even as I am using it. I am not learning definitions as established in even the latest dictionary. I'm not a dictionary-maker. I'm a person a dictionary-maker has to contend with. I'm a living element in the development of language.

One of my favorite poems in your new book has that delightful combination of attitudes: pride, wonder, and utter humility. In "The Way I Write," the poem seems to declare that this activity is absolutely crucial to the universe and, at the same time, is completely insignificant. As if Dante, Jefferson, and Emily Dickinson are hanging on your words—"important / additions but immediately obsolete, like waves."

But this makes me think that if you write the way we have been talking about—the way I think I do, accepting what comes—then many of those poems will seem insignificant, and they *are* insignificant, and even ludicrous and grotesque to those who have "standards." [I'm] willing to look awkward when I try to catch one that can't be caught, to stumble because of the inability of language to get there from here. So I don't feel protective of the poems.

But, as readers, we can't easily dismiss this impulse as insignificant, maybe because we feel it within ourselves, maybe because you take the work so seriously. "The ocean and I have many pebbles / to find and wash off and roll into shape."

Yes, I think it is possible to take a stand that will enable you to laugh them off, but I guess what I'm saying is that the ocean finds them important. Me too.

But then there is a crucial pause in "The Way I Write," a questioning that stops your hand on the page.

My hand stops, and I don't put into the poem what could be after that question, because I'm not in the same universe as those people who think there's an answer. It doesn't stop arbitrarily, it doesn't stop whimsically; it stops necessarily. Well, Wittgenstein said, "Some questions shouldn't even be asked," and the implied answer that's in that space—there's nothing there. I don't know, that's the next poem.

Would it be far from the truth to say, then, that—whether we're talking about the elegies or the love poems—William Stafford's work is poetry of praise?

Yeah, I would be ready for that. Praise in the sense that it is an embracing of emerging experience. It is a participation in discovery. I am a butterfly, I'm not a butterfly collector. I want the experience of the butterfly.

Elemental Moves

An Interview with Michael Markee and
Vincent Wixon

1. Nothing Less than Everything

Would you comment on your poetic output?

Just a mountain of poems. Like the little mill that turned the sea
to salt. This is a consideration: reduce the output and up the
quality? Would it have worked that way, I wonder?

What about the pleasure of writing?

Well, it's like making remarks. You keep on. When you're at a
party you're in a conversation and you don't want to go back
and say, "Let's go stand back where we were before and see if I
can say that better." Instead you want to go on; you're pursuing
something. I feel I'm pursuing something in my writing. It's not
the same as thinking that every remark I make has to be crafted
for fear I might say something wrong. I'd just go ahead and say
something wrong and try to repair it later by saying something
that would take care of it.

   It does feel as if you could be a kind of committee inside
yourself. There's your self that tosses them off, then there's
your critical self, then there's your really mean and critical self.
Usually the self that I write my poems with is a conversational
self.

   It might be that if you looked at your jotting, your journal,
carefully enough you would find that you really are writing one
thing. You're just sort of turning it around and writing another
version. I take all of those versions and send them off as separate

poems. Maybe they're really trying to zero in on something that's like an abiding concern in yourself.

So you're saying it's possible that if you had been more critical you would sense more of the purpose?

There are the two parts of myself. There is a part of myself that thinks I could enhance anything I've written. It says, yeah, I think I can. Spending more time on one thing, I'd just work it over and work it over, would it get better? I think up to a point beyond where I usually go, it probably would, but I lose interest. I send it out as a remark rather than a milestone. So you might trade quantity for more quality. In fact, that's what people say— so and so writes too much. I can understand that rationale in back of what they're saying. If you'd keep it around might it be improved? It could be improved. I would readily agree to that. Might you improve it? That's possible. So why don't you, instead of sending things off to all of these places that need poems, why don't you hold the cards closer to your vest and not play them like this until there's a real bid. I don't know if it would work that way.

Would the pleasure have been as great?

I had a lot of fun sending those things out everywhere, all sorts of places. A magazine just came this week. The editor had written to me that it was a new venture. He asked if I would send some poems, which I did, which they took, which they published. Then I looked in the contributors' notes and it said something like this: "Unlike some other American poets, William Stafford does not try to keep from publishing in new ventures like ours," and that's nice. It sounds fine, but, actually, I think the reading public is benefited by the best possible magazines, not the most possible magazines.

I want to keep the line of thought I had about the pleasure of writing. When do you find that most—in the early stages, or in the whole process of writing and playing around with it, then typing it up and sending it out?

It's not the typing it up and sending it out that motivates me. It's the early part of the writing when something begins to happen. You discover something you hadn't known before, or you begin to have an experience in language that's new. It's that part. The revising I don't dread at all. It's interesting, but I think if you would calculate a writing career, which I never did, the maximum career would have put more time on brooding about what you have written and typed out, and I'm all too likely to get interested in the next thing. This is not finished—the old saying—it's abandoned. You've done it. There's another part that isn't at all honorific for me, but I'll confess it. I like to be the kind of person to whom a lot of things occur. I want to keep being like that.

It seems to me that you risk more by sending out a lot of poems rather than making a few crafted gems. For people who send out a few and keep working on poems for months and years, there's something less free about that.

Yes, there's another consideration I think of, though. If you work that way a long time and you send it out and it is rejected, you would really feel dejected. But if you send out a lot and a lot of them are rejected, you think, why not, another one is coming along and I can't really blame them for rejecting it. That's the way I feel. I'm not hurt by rejection, because what are they rejecting?—hardly anything! If I spent more time on each one, would I feel more hurt at the rejection of each one? Possibly.

How about major statements in general? I have the feeling that the estimate people put on their utterances is often ridiculous, and maybe I have a fear of giving into that stance myself. The feeling that *this* is worthy. . . . What does worthy mean? In an article I read that John Ciardi said, "Did they bounce?" to a student who'd written, "His eyes fell on the table." Well, that's a cute thing for Ciardi to say, but when a person is reading something, and I'm listening to them, trying to follow what they're trying to get at, I have a sympathy for their getting there. I'm trying to get there with them rather than pouncing like a hawk on the way they're doing it. For me the estimate that you'd make of your own quality, if you put a lot of effort in on it, would be too high.

What is quality? It depends on where you stand, whether you feel you're limited or not. I feel I'm limited. I feel other people are limited. This idea, whatever standard American writers have reached is estimable and other standards are not, is a relative matter. In a way, I could say I'm not that ambitious, but another way I could put it is I'm a lot more ambitious than that. I don't want to reach the standard that American poetry has reached. Nothing less than everything, that's what I would like to find by keeping going. The idea that you could cut back a little bit and thus be esteemed is not as important to me as if you could keep on being headlong, you might get beyond esteemed. I'd like that. So maybe I'm more ambitious. God has got bigger plans than the standards of American poetry, no matter what those standards are.

I'm suspicious of the ability of any fallible human being to erect some kind of standard and say, this is it. The realm of possibility is more glorious than that—that would be one way to put it. The closing in on some kind of hierarchy is a function of the limitedness of the judges more than it is the quality of the work. So I like the idea of operating in that playing field where it's not "tennis with the net down," as Frost said. Tennis isn't enough. The net could never be high enough. To play a game with it a certain height, then you can say you have done something in this limited game, but there are a lot of other things that are possible that we haven't conceived of. Just this morning I was trying to write about that. I think about the things I've accomplished, and then I think of the things I haven't had the sense to realize it would be possible to accomplish. A "What am I missing?" kind of feeling. For me writing is invading that area of "What am I missing?" rather than "Does this reach a standard?"

You live your life by the feeling of satisfaction a day at a time. Those who try to say, well, at least, no matter how grim this makes you feel to do this drudgery writing (a lot of writers talk this way), at least you have your accomplishment in the end. I don't feel that way at all. I feel the other way around. At least you have pleasant days. You have good feelings about your life. As far as what I've accomplished, I don't know.

The motivation I feel about writing is just the closures when you're doing it. It's not, "If I work today I'll have something to show someone tomorrow." It's more like the feeling I have if I go out hiking. What makes me scramble up the canyon and poke around everywhere is that I'm having experiences while I'm doing it. It isn't, "Then I can go back and report." I'm not thinking about that. I'm not hired to do it, and I'm not getting a reward for having done it. I'm doing it because it's a pleasure.

2. From Journal to Poem

Reading with Little Sister: A Recollection

The stars have died overhead in their great cold.
Beneath us the sled whispers along. Back there
our mother is gone. They tell us, "If you hold on
the dogs will take you home." And they tell us never
to cry. We'll die too, they say, if we
are ever afraid. All night we hold on.
The stars go down. We are never afraid.

This is a page [*holding up journal page*] that seemed fairly neat to me because something that started out meandering found its way by the end of the page almost in the form it was when it became a short poem that was published. The whole poem came out of "If we held on to the sled," and about how our father would pull us home, and then he wasn't in it and "our mother was gone," "the dogs would pull us home"—all sorts of things just came out in one page. And the page just didn't let go of itself. It started with what seemed random things and it never was fully developed, but instead the beginning was sort of turned onto itself and revised and added to and the next thing the same. Then pretty soon the whole thing seemed to be together.

Transcription of journal for 26 December 1986:

If we held onto the sled and if we didn't
cry, our father would pull us home. Huge
frozen drifts leaned over the road. Back there our mother
was lost [, was gone]. As we would be if we were afraid.
We held on.

The sled whispered along. They told us
if we held on the dogs would pull us
home. Huge frozen drifts loomed near.
They told us never to cry. Back there
our mother was gone. Somewhere ahead
a road would take us home. We'd die,
they said, if we were ever afraid.

Back there our mother is gone. [Under] Beneath us [all night]
    the sled
[the sled] whispers along. They tell us if we hold on
the dogs will [take] pull us home. Huge [frozen] drifts
loom near

[In their great cold] the stars have died overhead in their great
    cold.
Beneath us the sled whispers along. Back there
our mother is gone. They tell us if we hold on
the dogs will take us home. And they tell us never
to cry. We'll die too they say, if we
are ever afraid. All night we hold on.
The stars go down. We are never afraid.

What kept me turning this over and changing the order was
that the cadence wasn't going right and the way it is at the end
feels about right to me in terms of a long sentence, a shorter
sentence, a short sentence. Instead of "In their great cold the
stars have died overhead," it says "The stars have died over-
head in their great cold." And there was a part, "The sled
whispered along" that changes to "Beneath us the sled whispers
along." Sometimes when I've read this I've thought it seems so
simple . . . how easy it is to write. I say "The stars have died
overhead [*points up*] in their great cold. Beneath us [*points
down*] the sled whispers along. Back there [*gestures over his shoul-
der*] our mother is gone." I mean just elemental moves—just
here, here, here. It was that kind of placement and sequencing
and cadencing that I think my language was trying for as I let it
tumble on down the page.

The very last sentence seems a precipitous way to end the
poem and also a kind of a vaunting, but at the same time ner-
vous vaunting. "All night we hold on. The stars go down. We are

never afraid." As if when I wrote that or when I read it now I have this feeling: that's what the kids tell each other.

It's the kind of poem I would like to have circulated in the world. It's about something that is important to me and it just seems to be worth doing. Now it could be a little poem, something like "First Grade":

> In the play Amy didn't want to be
> anybody; so she managed the curtain.
> Sharon wanted to be Amy. But Sam
> wouldn't let anybody be anybody else—
> he said it was wrong. "All right," Steve said,
> "I'll be me, but I don't like it."
> So Amy was Amy, and we didn't have the play.
> And Sharon cried.

It feels like a significant part of the experience of life, the poem does. I was thinking of other little poems like "The Little Girl by the Fence at School":

> Grass that was moving found all shades of brown,
> moved them along, flowed autumn away
> galloping southward where summer had gone.
>
> And that was the morning someone's heart stopped
> and all became still. A girl said, "Forever?"
> And the grass: "Yes. Forever." While the sky—
>
> The sky—the sky—the sky.

I think that's a clinch central-content kind of thing. The content is coercive.

It's a feeling about the experience of life?

I guess so. I wish it were possible for me to engage in the big world discussion about what this means, but I'm not sure I can. Though when I'm on something worth doing it's a feeling, I guess. I'm going to try to justify that feeling. The content—no matter the position of the people involved or the claims of the content—it can brush against something that reverberates with everybody or with many people. "The Little Girl by the Fence at School" is a kind of absolute dead end: "and that was the day someone's heart stopped." Then it goes on. Or even this one about the sled, there's kind of a human adventure in this. It's bigger than just two little kids on a sled, or maybe that's as big as anything there is.

3. Making a List Poem

The Sparkle Depends on Flaws in the Diamond

Wood that can learn is no good for a bow.

The eye that can stand the sun can't
    see in shadow.

Fish don't find the channel—the channel
    finds them.

If the root doesn't trust, the plant
    won't blossom.

A dog that knows jaguars is no longer
    useful in hunting.

You can lie at a banquet, but you have to
    be honest in the kitchen.

Priorities at Friday Ranch

1) All that cut juniper west of
    Lava Lake will yield fenceposts
    if you can get there before the crew
    has to clean up for summer.

2) The best tumbleweed you can find
    would look good, hung up for shadows
    about where Dave always put
    his hat by the barn light.

3) If you ever see that gray antelope
    again find out if it has a white
    foot—I think it had a white foot
    on the back left side.

Sayings of the Blind

Feeling is believing.

Mountains don't exist. But their slopes do.

Little people have low voices.

All things, even the rocks, make a little noise.

The silence back of all sound is called "the sky."

There's a big stranger in town every day called the sun.
    He doesn't speak to us but puts out a hand.

Night opens a door into a cellar.
    You can smell it coming.

On Sundays everyone stands farther apart.

Velvet feels black.

Meeting cement is never easy.

What do they mean when they say night is gloomy?

Edison didn't invent much.

Whenever you wake up it's morning.

Names have a flavor.

Things I Learned Last Week

    Ants, when they meet each other,
    usually pass on the right.

    Sometimes you can open a sticky
    door with your elbow.

    A man in Boston has dedicated himself
    to telling about injustice.
    For three thousand dollars he will
    come to your town and tell you about it.

    Schopenhauer was a pessimist but
    he played the flute.

    Yeats, Pound, and Eliot saw art as
    growing from other art. They studied that.

If I ever die, I'd like it to be
in the evening. That way, I'll have
all the dark to go with me, and no one
will see how I begin to hobble along.

In The Pentagon one person's job is to
take pins out of towns, hills, and fields,
and then save the pins for later.

Would you comment on the making of "Things I Learned Last Week"?

Yes, I think I can. There's something in me that likes to start a
poem without fanfare, but with something happening. For me
the beginning of a poem would be "Sometimes I breathe." A
person might think, "What's going on? Of course sometimes you
breathe." But there's a kind of a promise. And here this:

Ants, when they meet each other,
usually pass on the right.

I think it sort of sets the tone for this poem. You don't know
whether to believe it or not, or what the significance is, but
there's something.

Dorothy and I were out hiking and we saw an anthill. They're
so busy, you know. And I looked and I thought I could make a
study to see which side they pass on. It's like traffic. I didn't
bother to make a study. I just decided they usually pass on the
right. *[Laughs]* By the way, I once read this in a high school. And
those dutiful kids, when I read that, I saw them writing down,
"Ants usually pass on the right." This is what they were learning
from my lecture. I felt like a real faker. *[Laughs]* I was thinking
about driving. They seemed to be driving. They seemed to be in
traffic. You know these lines of ants.

And then other things that are like throwaway:

Sometimes you can open a sticky
door with your elbow.

That's a fairly low-level bit of discovery. I have to assume that
you know you're going through a door and you just give it a

whack. It isn't much. But I think it comes for me about the right place in the poem because it's early, and the persons still can't feel that they're hooked, but they're sort of hooked with that "ants when they meet each other." I hope their minds are still spinning just a little bit. And then this sort of slows it down, but something's got to happen soon. And then the next one hits them harder—the one about injustice. So I don't feel that a poem ought to be blockbusters all the way, but modulation is a good thing. Luckily, it is a good thing because, perforce, most of us can't do blockbusters all the time anyway.

> A man in Boston has dedicated himself
> to telling about injustice.
> For three thousand dollars he will
> come to your town and tell you about it.

When I read this, audiences think it's really funny. And they don't know what to make of

> Schopenhauer was a pessimist but
> he played the flute.

I just got that out of reading Nietzsche.

I think that aphorism is particularly nice. You don't really need to know Schopenhauer to get the idea of the contrast.

Yes. And it just happens to be true. And any implications are in the mind of the reader. I would like that. I would like it to be not my enforcing something, but my presenting something from which they get something. The activity of the reader is the life of the poem. Something like that.

But it's orchestrated.

Yes, it's orchestrated, but people can feel noncoerced by the language and just sort of invited by the language and have the feeling of making a discovery.

> Yeats, Pound, and Eliot saw art
> as growing from other art. They studied that.

I want to hurry on when I say that. I don't want to stop and argue with those scholars whose eyebrows go up. "Well, you know, what else?" But I'm not saying anything, just going on.

Would you comment on the structure of that stanza—the implication of making it two sentences?

I wanted the first sentence to say something that many people, most people, maybe almost all people, maybe everyone but me would say, "Yeah. Yeats, Pound, and Eliot saw art as growing from other art." That's what art schools are. That's what critics say. That's what teachers say. That's what most poets, most writers say. I don't say that. But I don't say I don't say that. All I say is, "They studied that," and just leave them there sort of, "Oh, is it possible just to say something neutral like this about that?" Not say, "Of course," and I'm not about to say they're wrong. In fact they're so far wrong, I don't even say they're wrong. I say "They studied that," as if "Imagine!"

It's a pretty strong implication.

That's true. I just feel it's a delicious implication, but I feel sort of bullying or too much like a bull terrier to tangle with it, so I just observe it. Suddenly you see that's what they're doing. Before you just thought they're doing what everybody's doing. Or what everybody has to do. Suddenly you see, "Oh that's something *they* do." Which means there might be something else to do. *[Laughs]*

And one I really like: "If I ever die . . ." That's sort of like "Sometimes I breathe." And the stinger at the end.

It would be a much different poem if you ended with the "hobble along" section.

I think it would. I think that throughout there is an attempt to make these alternate along. You know, sort of coercive things. "If I ever die" or "In The Pentagon" or the man dedicating

43

himself to justice with insulation between them. So the whole poem has the same flavor as the title. It's just "Things I Learned Last Week." It doesn't say important things, or unimportant things. These are just a succession of things—I want to keep it from being climactic or anticlimactic—just a succession of things the way the world gives you things.

The direction that some of those lead, like the Pentagon stanza, is pretty clear, or the reader has a sense of the speaker's feeling.

I think that's right, but suddenly I have a gust of ambition. I would like what the speaker or writer gives to the reader to be something so implicationful that the reader can't escape it. For all I know there is someone in the Pentagon, except they probably throw the pins away. *[Laughs]* But there could be someone, a frugal person like me. You know, I save the pins for later. It doesn't say what for. It just says, well, after all, they've been to towns, hills, and fields. What are they saving for later, and where am I going to be, sort of feeling. The Pentagon. That's the kind of place the Pentagon is.

Well, the "for later" to me is ominous. Isn't it to you?

Again and again and again. Until we've all had it. I think it's a kind of feeling. Of course, I don't think I violated what the Pentagon's about. They do put pins in towns, hills, and fields.

Now in your Daily Writing, your original entry goes farther, and says something about "after the world's destroyed . . ."

Yes, I don't say that in the poem, because again, the poem is just things I learned last week. I feel a kind of balance in each one of these things. It's not asserting too much, and it may not even be significant. But the very fact that you think it might be significant is significant. Each time. How about the person who is going to tell about injustice for three thousand dollars? That's as real as the Pentagon. That's exactly what they do. So why do you have a funny feeling? It's not my fault. I'm just telling you the way it is. *[Laughs]*

When you introduced this poem at the Library of Congress and other times too, I think you said, "It's the perfect kind of poem for a person like me."

Yes, that's right. You don't have to be well organized or anything. Though I think it is organized. But it just seems to be an aggregation of things to say.

Can you say something about what you chose to keep in and what you chose not to include in this poem? You had a lot of other material in your Daily Writings you could have included.

I think partly it was space. This is not a big poem and though I did have the feeling when I was writing it, putting these things together—in fact since then—I can make it go on and on. It's the kind of thing that you could just keep saying. But I think once it has a certain length, a certain number of these that established the tonality and balance, that's enough, I had the feeling. Especially when I was able to come out of it with the two—"If I ever die" and "In The Pentagon"—that's about as serious as I'm going to get it, and there's no need in going on with other little aphorisms in the journal like "What you can make with a knife you can mar with a knife," or "Wood that can learn is no good for a bow," though I think that's kind of a nice little idea, but nice ideas are not enough. The poem's got to have a kind of trajectory, and I just thought it had it.

"Nothing Less than Everything," *Oregon English Journal,* spring 1994; portions of "Elemental Moves 1, 2, and 3" used in *William Stafford, The Life of the Poem,* TTTD Productions, 1992, videocassette; "Reading with Little Sister: A Recollection," from *Passwords* (New York: Harper-Perennial, 1991); "First Grade," from *An Oregon Message* (New York: Harper and Row, 1987); "The Little Girl by the Fence at School," from *Stories That Could Be True* (New York: Harper and Row, 1977); "The Sparkle Depends on Flaws in the Diamond," from *An Oregon Message* (New York: Harper and Row, 1987); "Priorities at Friday Ranch," from *My Name Is William Tell* (Lewiston, ID: Confluence Press, 1992); "Sayings of the Blind," unpublished, February 18, 1993; "Things I Learned Last Week," from *A Glass Face in the Rain* (New York: Harper and Row, 1982).

II
Encounters with Poetry

An Afternoon in the Stacks

Closing the book, I find I have left my head
inside. It is dark in here, but the chapters open
their beautiful spaces and give a rustling sound,
words adjusting themselves to their meaning.
Long passages open at successive pages. An echo,
continuous from the title onward, hums
behind me. From in here the world looms,
a jungle redeemed by these linked sentences
carved out when an author traveled and a reader
kept the way open. When this book ends
I will pull it inside-out like a sock
and throw it back in the library. But the rumor
of it will haunt all that follows in my life.
A candleflame in Tibet leans when I move.

From *Passwords* (New York: HarperPerennial, 1991).

Roethke's Way

Theodore Roethke's students witness that he liked to require practice in standard forms. This witness helps to account for the combined originality and decorum of his poems. He starts from regularity and makes forays from it.

One might say that free verse is written by an out-group reaching in or an in-group reaching out. Roethke was of the latter kind. He knew where the pattern was but was ready to reach outward. He taught his students so, and was himself, like a master of the Japanese brushstroke: the effect looks casual, but the moves come from practice backed by childhood use of chopsticks.

Roethke's work shows two ways of forming a poem. Some are crisply regular:

> The anger will endure,
> The deed will speak the truth
> In language strict and pure,
> I stop the lying mouth:
> Rage warps my clearest cry
> To witless agony.

Others are flourishing departures from regularity:

> Winding upward toward the stream with its sharp stones,
> The upland of alder and birchtrees,
> Through the swamp alive with quicksand,
> The way blocked at last by a fallen fir-tree,
> The thickets darkening,
> The ravines ugly.

Unpublished, 1966. Roethke quotations from *Open House* (New York: Doubleday, 1941) and *The Far Field* (New York: Doubleday, 1964).

This second example demonstrates two typical characteristics. One is that when Roethke departed from regular forms he tended to use a falling rhythm. Note the ending sounds of these lines—birchtrees, quicksand, fir-tree, darkening, ugly. And the one other—sharp stones—gives the Roethke nuance to the prevalent beat; the voice can hover. This lilt appears throughout his work, and is in fact so pervasive that one could feel uncomfortable about bringing it into clear notice. Roethke's pattern, his characteristic manner, fits the falling rhythm so neatly that he sometimes appears to be fitting out English for conformity to some foreign language, like Italian. He flirts with long patches of systematically distorted rhythms. He speaks English to that different drummer, the one with limber drumsticks.

The other characteristic demonstrated by the second passage is Roethke's control of a pattern larger than the metrical and smaller than the stanza: he manages the excursions of the breath. He provides rests, slow places, and cumulative sequences. He programmed the requirements on the voice, so that what he was saying gained reinforcement in the rising or descending effort of the breath.

Finally, what strikes a reader most about the poems is their audacity. The content is wild and witty, and the sounds are quick, confident, witty experiments. The shapes that seem to spatter down on the page come to have a cherishable existence—little, hopping, limping, lovable shapes, they whistle and scamper. Their maker lived with them, loved them; they are God's creatures, all. Witness the last part of "The Geranium":

> Near the end, she seemed almost to hear me—
> And that was scary—
> So when that snuffling cretin of a maid
> Threw her, pot and all, into the trash-can,
> I said nothing.
>
> But I sacked the presumptuous hag the next week,
> I was that lonely.

Brother Antoninus—the World
as a Metaphor

The poetry of Brother Antoninus confronts the reader with two main hazards, the first an immediate and obvious quality, and the second a more pervasive demand. The immediate quality is that of bleakness and insistent emotional involvement, lying at an extreme from prettiness, and even from recent, more generously updated conceptions of poetry's content. Modern poetry is no valentine, but Brother Antoninus has done more than leave off the lace:

> the great elk, caught midway between two scissoring logs,
> Arched belly-up and died, the snapped spine
> Half torn out of his peeled back, his hind legs
> Jerking that gasped convulsion, the kick of spasmed life,
> Paunch plowed open, purple entrails
> Disgorged from the basketwork ribs
> Erupting out, splashed sideways, wrapping him,
> Gouted in blood, flecked with the brittle sliver of bone.
>
> ("In All These Acts")

This passage is from a late, religious poem, and in the development of Brother Antoninus's work it seems that the more intense his religious commitment becomes, the more violent the content of his poetry.

This bleak aspect of the work impressed critics from the first. Kenneth Rexroth, in an article which helped to launch "the beat

From the introduction to *The Achievement of Brother Antoninus* (Glenview, IL: Scott, Foresman, 1967).

generation" into public notice ("San Francisco Letter," in the second issue of *Evergreen Review*), calls William Everson "probably the most profoundly moving and durable poet of the San Francisco Renaissance," and continues: "His work has a gnarled, even tortured honesty, a rugged unliterary diction, a relentless probing and searching, which are not just engaging, but almost overwhelming." And Rexroth goes on to say, "Anything less like the verse of the fashionable literary quarterlies would be hard to imagine." The implication is meant to be honorific: "rugged unliterary diction," not like "the verse of the fashionable quarterlies." But that implication, though understandable, is quite misleading. Rugged as the poems are, they are lavishly literary.

Consider the organization of sound in the following passages. The striking words and pictures may pose as unliterary but are in fact elaborate with repeated sounds and varied, rhymed, slurred progressions:

> They came out of the sun with their guns geared,
> Saw the soft and easy shape of that island
> Laid on the sea,
> An unwakening woman,
> Its deep hollows and its flowing folds
> Veiled in the garland of its morning mists.
>
> ("The Raid")

> "No pride!" cried God, "kick me I come back!
> Spit on me I eat your spittle!
> I crawl on my belly!"
>
> ("A Frost Lay White on California")

It is clear that the immediate quality of bleakness and shock looms here, but everything is tuned and heightened and artful, even relentlessly artful. Consider the syllables and their sounds, no matter where they come in the lines, no matter how casually they seem to fall—the sun-gun-geared of the first line, the saw-soft, easy-shape of the second line. Think of the hovering erotic implication of the scene in "The Raid." How could you find in any "fashionable quarterly" any verse with more density of repetition than pride-cried-God-kick-come-back? The reader may trust his sense of something special in the language of these poems;

they are both rugged *and* literary. The immediate quality of feeling, the shock, derives from something other than just rough words, and in order to identify the cause of the obvious bleakness and shock, we must cast back to the first statement made about the self, the persona, which is created out of contrasts.

One kind of poetry—and the poetry of Brother Antoninus is a distinguished example of it—flourishes because it expresses many impulses which practical, politic life coerces most of us to avoid. That is, many of our everyday actions and sayings we adjust to calculations about effects on others; we are purposeful and instrumental with language. But there is another way to live, a way to stay honest without staying silent; and the poetry of Brother Antoninus demonstrates this other way—it is a shock and a delight to break free into the heart's unmanaged impulses. All literature lives in one way or another with this freedom, but the Everson-Antoninus poetry lives openly—even flagrantly—by continual recourse to shock.

Brother Antoninus has committed his whole life to conduct and communication that maintain independence, a stance of accepting what the immediate being can find, and a readiness to reject anything else; he is a passionate romantic. As a radical in politics, as a conscientious objector in war, as a recklessly individual spokesman in his religion, Everson-Antoninus exemplifies to an extreme degree a quality which marks current literature— the exhilaration of rebellion. A reader must accept a certain view if he is to read such a writer sympathetically; he must relish how the literature stiff-arms the genteel, how the author delights in presenting abruptly topics often avoided. Brother Antoninus requires this kind of acceptance immediately and repeatedly.

The shock method is evident in the following passages, chosen from early and late work. Note that the passages do not necessarily prove anything unusual, nor do they have to consist of inherently shocking materials; but each one deliberately confronts the reader with a certain almost electric realization that the writer has shoved against commonly slurred-over or conventionalized human expectations. After an introductory poem, the selection in this text begins with the line: "These verses are lies." Immediately the writer has begun his attack on the reader's expectations. The following demonstrate the prevalence of this

challenge as a way of writing; the author subjects his reader to a
world that hurts:

> When they rode that hawk-hearted Murietta down in the
>   western hills
> They cut the head loose to prove the bounty.
>
> ("Lines for the Last of a Gold Town")

> He is a god who smiles blindly,
> And hears nothing, and squats faun-mouthed on the wheeling
>   world.
>
> ("Circumstance")

> Churchill: the sound of your voice from the eastern air. . . .
> Who listen beyond the hammering tongue
> for the eloquent fallacy wound at its root
> Are not to be wooed.
>
> ("The Unkillable Knowledge")

These are typical passages. They demonstrate the punishing
quality in the poems: the reader is to suffer while he receives
something that promises an eventual, bitter, satisfying reward.

Bleak, rugged passages, though extreme in the work of Brother
Antoninus, and hence an immediate hazard to some readers, do
not constitute so much a barrier as does his other main distinc-
tion. That quality is, bluntly put, didacticism. Brother Antoninus
takes a conspicuously unfashionable stand on the issues of belief,
assertion, and authority in literature. The results of his stand
pervade his poems, which consequently baffle or estrange some
readers.

We are accustomed today to accept for the duration of a
literary experience all kinds of moral reversals, antiuniverses,
and ordinarily outrageous assumptions. We ride with the work,
accepting the author's most emphatic statements temporarily,
without yielding ourselves in any vital way to his assumed author-
ity. We accept his tone as part of the literary experience, but we
know that the writer cannot through personal authority coerce
our belief. He can only provide us with experiences which we
can value for their shimmer and excitement. The fine arts can-
not impose; they have to appeal.

However, a generation ago, or longer, an author was a sage, sometimes almost a prophet, a model of some kind; Brother Antoninus is in that tradition, and his poems take on a prophetic, oracular tone. What he presents, he presents as an insight, a truth, not merely as an exercise of the imagination. In his work his voice is direct; he does not turn aside to flirt with fancies and baffling temporary allegiances; there is no Emperor of Ice Cream in his poetry, no Raven saying "Nevermore" to enhance a temporary feeling chosen for literary exercise. Brother Antoninus sets up to be a thinker and guide, a statesman of letters. His stance is that of responsibility. "These verses are lies," yes; but only because they come from a limited intelligence and will, not because the writer is setting out to create passing sensations for the reader.

So the reader of Everson-Antoninus finds himself presented with metaphors intended as truth. The world that is asserted must be linked in its largest events and in its details with a belief that is asserted triumphantly, but then subjected to the terrors and horrors and weaknesses of our existence, and then asserted again. It is the vicissitudes of this faith, surviving in the modern world and in the particulars of the author's life, that have become more and more central in the work of Brother Antoninus.

Even his earlier work is tied to the soul's program of development: his poetry inducted him into his religion, and his religion shapes his poetry. The reader who is unwilling to accept that pattern, who is reluctant to suspend his disbelief in the significance of the particulars of the author's life as the author sees them, will be continually under a strain in reading the poetry; for it asks the reader's participation and makes the author's discoveries into the central rewards of the later poems:

> And I crawl.
> I will get there.
> Like a clubbed snake
> I hitch toward freedom.
> Out of this skin, this slough,
> Across these illusions,
> Upon this blood.
>
> ("The Face I Know")

In addition to the evidence in poem after poem that Brother Antoninus is using literature deliberately for purposes other than just the literary, the author himself, outside his poems, declares his objectives. He says in a letter about his work, "I strive for spiritual perfection and make the striving the subject and the themes of my poetry." The foreword to his 1962 collection, *The Hazards of Holiness*, elaborates:

> This is not to say that I despise craftsmanship, but only that the struggle with language is the struggle to make myself comprehensible to myself, or orient my inner and outer being. . . .
>
> Thus I can truthfully say that I have no interest in the conquest of language, as understood by those who seek to achieve a hypostatized aesthetic object. The victories I seek, those of "appeasement and absolution, and something very near to annihilation," are one and all victories over myself, the unremitting attempt to exorcize the demon.

Important as the author's attitude is, and pervasive as its effect is, in the work of Brother Antoninus, the disclaimer of literary ambition need not greatly change the reader's approach. For Brother Antoninus—whatever his explicit intention—is manifestly and even almost helplessly poetic. He maintains creative momentum partly because he continues to be surprised at his own religiousness; he continues to make the kind of visionary statement a discoverer makes. The world says straight to him what it is supposed to say, and for the reader it is the intensity, rather than the validity, of the statements that counts. Almost to the pitch of a Saint Francis, Brother Antoninus encounters the intricate sermons of God acted out by the creatures around us:

> Curlews, stilts and scissortails, beachcomber gulls,
> Wave-haunters, shore-keepers, rockhead-holders, all cape-top
>   vigilantes,
> Now give God praise.
> Send up the articulation of your throats
> And say His name.
>
> ("A Canticle to the Water Birds")

It is difficult to overstate the alienation this writer works from; he gives ordinary readers a view of the place of the absolutist, of the principled rebel. This is not to say that his stance is one of moral superiority; but he has taken the much-contemplated step of saying no to the state, and has been imprisoned for it. That passionate individuality referred to earlier resulted in long-suffering rebellion, in circumstances which continue to test individual values. It is unlikely that many readers even today can participate emotionally, without some qualms, in such a poem as "The Unkillable Knowledge" or, as expressed more simply, in this passage from "The Vow":

> I flinch in the guilt of what I am,
> Seeing the poised heap of this time
> Break like a wave.
> And I vow not to wantonly ever take life;
> Not in pleasure or sport,
> Nor in hate . . .
> And seek to atone in my own soul
> What was poured from my past.

This pronounced alienation from the "national purpose" when the main group of citizens were mobilized for war has marked one section of our society, and the work of Brother Antoninus is in regard to pacifism probably the most representative of all that the "Beat" poets of the San Francisco group have produced. After World War II the Bay Area in California became a center for many who had been uprooted and had come to know the attractions of the place. Brother Antoninus—then William Everson—had been a prisoner in isolated Civilian Public Service camps during the war years, and he had seen many of his friends taken away to prison. The society around him was alien enough to bring about in-group solidarity among the students, conscientious objectors, and political radicals who began to identify themselves and each other during the postwar years. That background of disaffection with a warring society is worth mention in order to point out that the literary renaissance in San Francisco, as well as later campus and political events of the Bay Area, stems partly from the kind of position exemplified by this poet. . . .

If I Could Be Like Wallace Stevens

The octopus would be my model—
it wants to understand; it prowls
the rocks a hundred ways and holds
its head aloof but not ignoring.
All its fingers value what
they find. "I'd rather know," they say,
"I'd rather slime along than be heroic."

My pride would be to find out; I'd
bow to see, play the fool,
ask, beg, retreat like a wave—
but somewhere deep I'd hold the pearl,
never tell. "Mr. Charley,"
I'd say, "talk some more. Boast again."
And I'd play the banjo and sing.

From *A Glass Face in the Rain* (New York: Harper and Row, 1982).

Emily

On that page where the whole world moved
and other people ran
frantic in their lives to stay the same,
she was the stillest one—

Eye in the night to lag or surge,
ready to catch the shine
of the newest star or the old sky in the brain
where the right word again begins time.

From Marguerite Harris, ed., *Emily Dickinson: Letters from the World* (New York: Corinth Books, 1970).

In Memoriam
Richard Hugo, 1923–1982

Fame of a special kind—narrow, but very intense—had come to Richard Hugo at the end of his life. During the succession of illnesses that preceded his death last month, he and his health were monitored by his band of admirers through telephone calls and notes, and then out along a network of information back and forth among themselves.

From his bed in Virginia Mason Hospital, Hugo stayed his characteristic self—in a strong voice, he joked about solemn things: "God—I'm fifty-nine years old—this is getting serious!" His wife, Ripley, was on hand while Hugo conducted the drama of his life with expressions of sympathy, excitement, and wry complaint—keeping in touch.

Among the poets, even though he was one of the most approachable of people, he was regarded with awe: he had been a technical writer for Boeing; he had played baseball; he had drunk with many a hearty companion, and caught fish in streams with wonderful names. And his poems delivered, with accuracy and fervor, those parts of his life.

A strange figure for a poet, to most people, he was burly and gruff. His poems had a thump to them; and he read to large, appreciative audiences with an extra emphasis, not disguising the straight, hard-driving lines. It would be hard to call their cadences graceful, but their meaning was graceful. Their steady, caring perceptivity was graceful.

In his breezy, risky way, he allowed what he said and wrote to

From *Seattle Weekly,* November 10, 1982.

lurch around and surprise people. His prose, for instance, is stealthily artful—in an elbowy way. He was not afraid to make abrupt commitments, and then to refine on them. When he wrote about Theodore Roethke as teacher—almost an idol among Northwest writers—there was no obeisance to the master: "Sometimes he read poems aloud and then couldn't explicate them clearly when he tried. I think he often didn't understand much of what he read." This offhand judgment is from a chapter of Hugo's *The Triggering Town* (about the craft of writing), in which Roethke is being lavishly credited for particular accomplishments—but not for all accomplishments.

Hugo's fame among poets began when he was lured from his job at Boeing in the early 1960s by Warren Carrier, the Wyatt Earp of the English department at the University of Montana, hired to ride in and bring order to what had been chaos. Hugo taught writing there and flourished—"Professor of Poetry," he chortled. And generations of students drifted into his aura in Missoula, off the ranches and reservations, even from the East; and once in the spell of Rattlesnake Canyon and the circle of writers in Missoula, they eddied around, reluctant to forsake the atmosphere created for artists in that environment.

The heavy, shambling spirit was Hugo, who conducted excited conversations about craft and substance in class—and around the bottle on the kitchen table in his old house near the campus, besieged by Montana storms, but made cozy by pictures, messages, clippings, broadsides, recipes, manuscripts of poems, reminders, and odd indecipherable scraps of paper tacked, nailed, clipped, pasted, wired, hooked, and magnetized to cupboards, walls, refrigerator, and stove.

What was it that entranced this life for those who came to know it? Richard Hugo had learned how to savor loneliness, how to salvage lives and at the same time to celebrate failure and neglect. He put a tang of sweetness into the spectacle of sadness. Students could fail and succeed in an atmosphere of acceptance. A champion of slobs and losers, Hugo balanced pity and love while doing his own awkward dance of existence.

To see him caring for his guests was to realize a new level of generosity. With what a wistful, piteous concern he peered into the refrig at night, fearful that the stores might close and leave the party lacking in ice cream!

In later years, Hugo could no longer claim failure and loneliness. He and his wife, Ripley ("My marriage has brought me such happiness that it is depriving me of the sorrows and images that enlivened my writings"), entertained streams of grateful writers in their home. The two of them traveled—a year on the Isle of Skye, a revisiting of Italy, where Dick traversed and vibrated to the scenes of his service on a bombing plane in World War II. And when they came back it was to reading circuits, prizes, a post as judge of the Yale Series of Younger Poets.

He couldn't claim failure and loneliness any more.

But he never forgot where those companions of his earlier years had been, and where they lurked still, for himself and for everyone. The power of his stance—and the abiding quality in his poems—comes from a perception that never wavered: each person has need; each person will die; each person stares out of a story full of suspense and surrounded by mystery.

Book Review: Keats's Poems

It is not casual and meaningless, the way
someone puts down a book or takes it up—
there are forces other than weight and momentum.
This book struggles in my hands. When I
tried to edge it onto a table it fell on the
floor dragging a magazine with it, and
a coffee spoon. I do not trust it. Though it
violates no law, it has an air of needing
watching—the lines test each other. They
belong where they are, but give signs of
elsewhere and other. The author may be
dependable, even rigidly respectable, but
he seems to know something—something that
makes even con men naive. All the time I was
reading it, I heard a warning, a little alarm.

From *You and Some Other Characters* (Rexburg, ID: Honeybrook Press, 1987).

A Poet with Something to Tell You
On Philip Levine's Poetry

One way to get the immediacy of Philip Levine's poetry is to imagine overhearing it, maybe from the other side of a door, so that the strange *onwardness* of the language can snag you without the distraction of knowing it is poetry. Listen to this part of "No One Remembers," from *The Names of the Lost:*

> You think because I was a boy, I didn't hear, you think
> because you had a pocketful of loose change, your feet on
> the desk, your own phone, a yellow car on credit, I didn't
> see you open your hands like a prayer and die into them the
> way a child dies into a razor, black hair, into a tire iron, a
> chain. You think I didn't smell the sweat that rose from
> your bed, didn't know you on the stairs in the dark, grunting
> into a frightened girl. Because you could push me aside like
> a kitchen chair and hit where you wanted, you think I was a
> wren, a mourning dove surrendering the nest.

Philip Levine's messages to the world can be lined out this way, as prose, to demonstrate how easily this current poetry has pulled up alongside us and begun to deliver its immediately available communication—direct, uncluttered, nonesoteric. This kind of poetry—and Philip Levine is demonstrating it at its best year after year—doesn't require any background of culture from T. S. Eliot's "tradition," or even from the assumed centrality of the American Standard Background, as in Lowell's early work.

Levine's work quietly appropriates the direct language of

From *Inquiry,* June 26, 1978.

prose while maintaining a readiness to gain from the frequent
bonuses that lurk in syllables and cadences in the lingo of talk.
There is an immediate, coercive drop onto common experi-
ence, the opposite of scholarly allusion. But there is a kind of
unfolding and controlled tenacity about the sentences as they
go down the page. Here is the end of the poem quoted above,
this time by the lines as Philip Levine formed them:

> The earth is asleep, Joe,
> it's rock, steel, ice,
> the earth doesn't care
> or forgive. No one remembers
> your eyes before they tired,
> the way you fought weeping.
> No one remembers how much
> it cost to drive all night
> to Chicago, how much
> to sleep all night in a car,
> to have it all except
> the money. No one remembers
> your hand, opened, warm
> and sweating on the back
> of my neck when you first
> picked me up and said
> my name, *Philip,* and held
> the winter sun up
> for me to see outside
> the French windows of
> the old house on Pingree,
> no one remembers.

One shouldn't claim too much for these unspectacular lines, or
try to force admiration for an art that depends, after all, on
little, sustained satisfactions. But when the quietness and consis-
tency of a book like *The Names of the Lost* can recur to you as you
rove through other books, you begin to know that a voice has
established itself in your life. And you go back, wondering why it
is when "No one remembers" that you remember. You find
again a certain bittersweet flavor.

That flavor comes, it seems to me, from a distinctive inward
complexity in our time. For Levine, and for many, many others

today, the world is an unfeeling place. People brush on by, and forget. And we are surrounded by violence and foreshadowings. How can people be this way? And yet, it is only by our feelings that we identify "unfeeling." If the feelings didn't exist, there would be no reaction, no realization. In such a world, justice is a continent always being discovered by taking soundings. That continent comes into being as we read writers like Philip Levine. The tradition behind these individual talents is just the widely available tradition of being alive, of having relatives, of experiencing cold, hunger, fulfillment, loss, redemption. The places and people in these poems are there—inevitably—for all of us. They are the elements of our lives made clear, enhanced by art, and returned to us. In light of such poems we see better where we are now.

Levine is one of the many in this current tradition-of-being-alive. Many poets now do it his way—coming at experience with language validated by everyone's feelings about talk.

And sometimes his poems seem strange. I can't account for why they work: there are elements in each one not yet encompassed in critical theory. For example, in a poem called "Waiting," the reader finds a constant stretching toward particulars that are so incidental that they need not be explained, but so meaningful to the speaker that he must mention them:

> You sit
> at the window above the windswept yard
> treeless forever, and you pray
> for us all, for the lying witness
> left in a ditch, for the stolen car.

Any example may be forced under some critical formulation, but the effect of reading Levine is that of finding ourselves surprised by a move that carried us beyond what we knew, or where we have been, or where we expected to go.

Philip Levine is exploring, taking soundings. In such writing, even though people and places are nearby and the language is the language of talk, there can be many surprises. And when he does range into world events, his lines catch up occasional accelerations, recurrences at odd places, glimpses that allow ordinary phrases to go telescopic. A good example is found in "For the Poets of Chile" (also from *The Names of the Lost*). He remarks that "someone must / stand at the window . . . / remembering how once / there were voices." And speaking of "Victor, who died / on the third day," he ends with the living:

> Victor left a child,
> a little girl
> who must waken each day
> before her mother
> beside her, and dress
> herself in the clothes
> laid out the night
> before. The house sleeps
> except for her, the floors
> and cupboards cry out
> like dreamers. She goes
> to the table and sets out
> two forks, two spoons, two knives,
> white linen napkins gone
> gray at the edges,
> the bare plates,
> and the tall glasses
> for the milk they must
> drink each morning.

It was Ezra Pound, I believe, who said that poetry should be as well written as prose. To test whether Levine has something to tell you, regardless of how it is placed on the page, here is "On the Murder of Lieutenant José Del Castillo by the Falangist Bravo Martinez, July 12, 1936," printed as a news account:

When the Lieutenant of the Guardia de Asalto heard the automatic go off, he turned and took the second shot just above the sternum, the third tore away the right shoulder of his uniform, the fourth perforated his cheek. As he slid out of his comrade's hold toward the gray cement of the Ramblas he lost count and knew only that he would not die and that the blue sky smudged with clouds was not heaven for heaven was nowhere and in his eyes slowly filling with their own light. The pigeons that spotted the cold floor of Barcelona rose as he sank below the waves of silence crashing on the far shores of his legs, growing faint and watery. His hands opened a last time to receive the benedictions of automobile exhaust and rain and the rain of soot. His mouth, that would never again say "I am afraid," closed on nothing. The old grandfather hawking daisies at his stand pressed a handkerchief against his lips and turned his eyes away before they held the eyes of a gunman. The shepherd dogs on sale howled in their cages and turned in circles. There is more to be said, but by someone who has suffered and died for his sister the earth and his brothers the beasts and the trees. The Lieutenant can hear it, the prayer that comes on the voices of water, today or yesterday, from Chicago or Valladolid, and hangs like smoke above this street he won't walk as a man ever again.

Suddenly Everything Became Clear to Him

Remembering Raymond Carver

Well, for more than three years it was a picnic at Port Angeles. Raymond Carver got a grant and moved out from Syracuse with his friend Tess Gallagher, and they both poured out stories and poems, and Raymond's work, already much admired, took on a luster that will shine for a long time. And then in early August of this year he died.

Toward the last the stories and poems came racing at him. It was as if he had a big cookie cutter and could press it down on life anywhere and come up with something unexpected, unforeseen, miraculous. He snapped the camera on whatever he brought into focus and there it was—that's us. That's us? Oh, no. But, yes, come to think of it, yes. Alas.

What are these productions like? Here is a typical one in first person, about a family member, verging easily from everyday events and going out, out—to crash at the end:

Where the Groceries Went

When his mother called for the second time
that day, she said:
"I don't have any strength left. I want
to lay down all the time."

"Did you take your iron?" he wanted to know.
He sincerely wanted to know. Praying daily,
hopelessly, that iron might make a difference.

From *Washington Magazine,* November 1988.

"Yes, but it just makes me hungry. And I don't
have anything to eat."

He pointed out to her they'd shopped
for hours that morning. Brought home
eighty dollars' worth of food to stack
in her cupboards and the fridge.
"There's nothing to eat in this goddamn house
but baloney and cheese," she said.
Her voice shook with anger. "Nothing!"
"And how's your cat? How's Kitty doing?"
His own voice shook. He needed
to get off this subject of food; it never
brought them anything but grief.

"Kitty," his mother said. "Here, Kitty.
Kitty, Kitty. She won't answer me, honey.
I don't know this for sure, but I think
she jumped into the washing machine
when I was about to do a load. And before I forget,
that machine's making
a banging noise. I think there's something
the matter with it. Kitty! She won't
answer me. Honey, I'm afraid.
I'm afraid of everything. Help me, please.
Then you can go back to whatever it was
you were doing. Whatever
it was that was so important
I had to take the trouble
to bring you into this world."

Typically, this poem is a narrative and is like another poem,
"Mother." But different. And the same kind of materials gets
into the short stories. It's as if something out there in the world
is pounding to get into print and Raymond Carver is the one
who has to let it come. All the pieces have plenty of who-what-
when-where, but they also hold a stored-up accusation: "Why?"
Why does life have to be like this?

So from a house looking over the water there at Port Angeles
these stories and poems came tumbling, for Carver the writer,
after several other lives—and as he says somewhere, some times
in between. The good life apparently was finally his: "I'm living

the life that as a young writer I often dreamed about but never in my wildest imaginings thought could come true."

He didn't hold with the experimental writing of the sixties and seventies, and along with some other current authors he brought back narrative, straight realistic narrative, to both stories and poems. And it was the poems that surprised him; they came in bunches, a bookful at a time. He would have an uninterrupted interval in his house above the water and would turn out a series drawn out of his life, his present life, and out of those memories. . . .

He never left those memories of the bad times, family breakup, alcohol, hardscrabble jobs.

The flavor of this work is unmistakable, but it is hard to convey. For one thing, he did not approve of irony, but the events in his writings are ironic. He did not talk from a height about his characters: he was with the people he talked about. He felt as they did; he suffered, as they did; he was stupid, as they were. He abhorred anything "at the expense of someone else."

For those who knew him, such an attitude is not surprising. His manner was that of an intensely interested friend. He did not put himself at a distance; he couldn't. He was helplessly attached to being human. And it sometimes seemed that he could not even understand irony—for weren't we all vulnerable and weak? Don't these catastrophes—alcohol, bad marriages, nagging relatives—happen to everyone? He knew they did. The arrowlike directness of his writing came right out of his life and attitude. The conspiracy of an artist who took a view from on high was not for him.

In many interviews (he was obliging, and his talk about writing is spread everywhere for readers of large or small periodicals) he owned up to his practices, intuitions, limitations. His innocence was his strength—his readiness to be the person he naturally was and to assume that others were like that too.

Often a story and a poem will have the same basis, and often his enthusiasms will transfer—and be transfigured—in his writing. He cites a phrase from Chekhov that delights him: "suddenly everything became clear to him"; then somehow this surge of feeling carries over to the end of a poem called "Drinking While Driving" in which all that happens is casual, not important—"We do not have any place in mind to go, / we are just driving." But at the end the poem says, "Any minute now, something will happen."

Things do happen in his work, but they are routine things that come into intensity. Their context makes them sharp and clear and often barbed as a fishhook. In his essays on writing, which often appear to be fairly standard bits about craft, his illuminations flash forth. He denies the importance of talent, for instance, but says a writer needs "a unique and exact way of looking at things." His work is full of these snapshots of reality, these collages from experience that turn into art.

He says he loved the process of revision, but he goes on to say that his exacting revisions might spring from a disinclination to start anything new. He tumbled his ideas and phrases over and over till they became smooth; a handful of rocks turns into a collection of gems.

Even when he moves into fantasy the fantasy collides with the everyday, as when he says, "At night the salmon move / out from the river and into town," and then has them avoiding the A&W and has them bumping against cable TV lines. Mostly the poems move along like that, bumping into TV lines and other ordinary things, but then coming at the end to some phrasing that electrifies all the rest, as in "The Other Life": "My wife is in the other half of this mobile home / making a case against me"; then the body of the poem has details, but telling bits ("The man who owns this unit tells me, / Don't leave your car here"); then the last two lines: "My wife goes on writing and weeping, / weeping and writing in our new kitchen." That word *new* releases the hovering intensity.

And it is the hovering, withheld parts that most distinguish Carver's work. He can tell more or communicate more because the mind is busy filling in the parts unsaid. We are drafted into an account in which every element is charged by the presence of quiet, patient implication. It is as if Carver is leaning toward us and watching our expressions to see if we are following him into the trance of contemplation about something too important to overwhelm with assertions: we have to see it for ourselves.

All through those troubled earlier years when finding time to write was almost impossible (hence his habit of doing short pieces, pieces he could turn out in snatches—and could perhaps get immediate pay, for he always needed that) he had clung to the idea that he was a writer. He scrambled for the little markets where as a teacher John Gardner told him, "this was where the best fiction was being published, and all of the poetry."

And so he had made it. Raymond Carver, winner of prizes, famous author, was dashing off letters to friends and publishing everywhere, in big magazines, yes, but also in the heroic little magazines—*Seneca Review, Northwest Review,* the *Ohio Review, Ploughshares, Zyzzyva, Scripsi* . . .

He had to write fast because it was all—all the sadness, and all the stabbing moments of happiness—coming to an end. He embraced it all in a late poem addressed to his writing and fishing friend Richard Ford; they are in a boat in the Strait and feel a breeze coming:

> I feel it fan my face and ears. Feel it
> ruffle my hair—sweeter, it seems,
> than any woman's fingers.
>
> Then turn my head and watch
> it move on down the Strait,
> driving waves before it.
>
> Leaving waves to flop against
> our hull. The birds going crazy now.
> Boat rocking from side to side.
>
> "Jesus," you say, "I never saw anything like it."
> "Richard," I say—
> "You'll never see that in Manhattan, my friend."

Jeffers

He is little now, less than a gull,
but the place on the Coast he glimpsed
for us is the right size. On Cape Kennedy
they prepare his proof,

His belief in the sound no one heard,
the flash without anyone to see;
greater than nations, the reason for nations
to be. And greater anyway.

We do not plan the desert, but be there,
take the unplanned for ours; irrelevant
people the fierce rocks ignore, we find
an exit in Jeffers' mind.

Myself, I belong in Wyoming, a state
that is all skyline, but what he invented
serves like a secret cell for many
saints in our time,

And all that guarded his kingdom—the tower,
the skull—have joined the ruins that have
always helped: dying was his all his life,
and the non-human ways.

More than his message, we feel his regard;
and who can oppose him?—except with pitiful
hands? Less than a gull,
man is an animal

That thinks it understands.

From *North by West* (Seattle, WA: Spring Rain Press, 1975).

The Current of Humanity

Carolyn Forché's Against Forgetting:
Twentieth-Century Poetry of Witness

Carolyn Forché has for long exemplified the poetry of witness
and collected it from around the world. Her book is big and
forthright and encompassing—too significant to circle around
lightly. And yet its very ambition, and the problems it has to
surmount, invite many questions.

About its ambition there is no doubt—eight hundred pages of
lament, pain, misery, protest, regret, anger. Forché's eighteen-
page introduction surveys our century's plentiful "dark times"
and the poetic witness about them:

> The volume is arranged in sections according to regions
> and major events, with historical head-notes. Within each
> section, poets appear in chronological order by date of
> birth, with biographical notes to illuminate the experience
> of extremity for each poet, and a selection of poetry from
> available works in the English originals or in translation.
> The criteria for inclusion were these: poets must have
> personally endured such conditions; they must be
> considered important to their national literatures; and their
> work, if not in English, must be available in quality
> translation.

What follows is a heavy book, awesome. Down its long de-
scent, circle by circle, the reader is led, not induced by pleasure,
but informed, confronted, loaded with fright, sympathy, out-

From *Hungry Mind Review* 28 (winter 1993–94).

rage. The *why* of the book seems to be that kind of informing and a resulting shake of the head and a resolve: "No more."

Guided by introductions with historical background for each section, the reader encounters fifteen of our century's darker pieces of history: "The Armenian Genocide (1909–1918)," "World War I," "Revolution and Repression in the Soviet Union," "The Spanish Civil War," "World War II," "The Holocaust," "Repression in Eastern and Central Europe," "War and Dictatorship in the Mediterranean," "The Indo-Pakistani Wars," "War in the Middle East," "Repression and Revolution in Latin America," "The Struggle for Civil Rights and Civil Liberties in the United States," "War in Korea and Vietnam," "Repression in Africa and the Struggle Against Apartheid in South Africa," and "Revolutions and the Struggle for Democracy in China."

So it's big, sweeping, and aimed. You can seek out your known favorite writers and also—with the help of Carolyn Forché's knowledgeable research—some discoveries. Bertolt Brecht is here, always good for some quirky angles. And Nazim Hikmet from his prison, reporting after a recital of deprivations, "I am happy," the kind of unexpected bonus that jerks the reader into admiring attention. And Cavafy is wryly here, waiting for the barbarians. These already acclaimed writers loom in the text; they test the worth of less-known, here-discovered writers. And there are some new winners, to be noted later.

But there are inherent problems in a collection like this. For instance, the individual glimpses that create the distinction of poetry put a strain on the thesis of the book; poems that buckle down to the thesis can hardly attain the shiver of the unexpected that distinguishes lively discourse. We can be informed; we can encounter the thoughts and emotions of significant people, the poets, the editor, the translators—but it takes something more to validate the poetry experience.

And there is the whole burden of poetry-and-translation to attenuate the effect of a world anthology. Despite the efforts of translators—and we are all enriched by their work—it was not till page 66, at the first poem originally in English, that the clear-as-a-bell sign of a poem appeared. It was Edward Thomas's "The Owl." There had been anguish on earlier pages, and no doubt worthy efforts ("Foreign hands have come and yanked out / the sublime rose of freedom, / which finally bloomed from the pains of your race"). But then came "The Owl":

> Downhill I came, hungry, and yet not starved;
> Cold, yet had heat within me that was proof
> Against the North wind; tired, yet so that rest
> Had seemed the sweetest thing under a roof.
>
> Then at the inn I had food, fire, and rest,
> Knowing how hungry, cold, and tired was I.
> All of the night was quite barred out except
> An owl's cry, a most melancholy cry.
>
> Shaken out long and clear upon the hill,
> No merry note, nor cause of merriment,
> But one telling me plain what I escaped
> And others had not, that night, as in I went.
>
> And salted was my food, and my repose,
> Salted and sobered, too, by the bird's voice
> Speaking for all who lay under the stars,
> Soldiers and poor, unable to rejoice.

Not that the only resounding poetry has to be in its original language. The favorites cited earlier come through in translation. Here is the irrepressible Brecht, in "To Those Born Later":

> Truly, I live in dark times!
> The guileless word is folly. A smooth forehead
> Suggests insensitivity. The man who laughs
> Has simply not yet had
> the terrible news.

And—ranging a little farther from such names as have become well known in anthologies—here is Salvatore Quasimodo with his "Man of My Time," a poem that could key an insight about issues in the whole collection:

> You are still the one with the stone and sling,
> man of my time. You were there in the cockpit,
> with evil wings, the sundials of death,
> —I have seen you—in the fire-chariot, at the gallows,
> at the torture wheels. I have seen you; it was you

with your knowledge precisely extermination-guided,
loveless, Christless. You have killed again
as before, as your fathers killed, as the beasts
killed when first they saw you.
And this blood smells as it did on the day
when the brother said to the other brother:
Let us go into the fields. And that chill, clinging echo
has reached down even to you, within your day.
Forget, O sons, the blood clouds
risen from earth, forget the fathers:
their tombs sink down in the ashes;
the black birds, the wind, cover over their hearts.

The balance, the wide view, the current of humanity flowing in this poem can test the contradictions inherent in *Against Forgetting*, or any collection so constituted: How can poetry yoke itself to a flat thesis? For poetry flourishes by staying alive to alternatives. Irony haunts it. The shimmer of new, unexpected realizations flows through its lines. Quasimodo's poem even breaks through and rebukes the anthology's thesis, when he says, "Forget, O sons, the blood clouds."

A further problem about achieving authenticity in a survey like this one lurks everywhere in the selections: quality is primary, but the need for wide representation puts a strain on that criterion. And how vividly do you have to suffer in order to qualify? And how many generalizations can you allow yourself as you attempt both speed of communication and the qualifiers that life's many particulars demand?

I feel a bump when the explanatory text says, "The Germans decided." All Germans? And similarly when Carolyn Forché says, "My new work seemed controversial to my American contemporaries." (Who, me?) The labels in the book, the assumptions, and the speed of assessment almost inevitable for a book with a thesis like this one, put a torque on me, snagged my attention, kept me wary of living on the emotional high of atrocity hunger.

Carl Sandburg mentions somewhere the value of having "a good forgettery." Nietzsche speaks of "the use and abuse of history." How heavily should we load up with the past? For how long? In what size doses? On whose terms? This book—at the same time it documents our century's abundance of the poetry of witness—rouses such questions.

A poet, a person, a fallible human being, has to step carefully through a puzzling world. We have to remember our own surges of anger, how we sometimes choose a country or a people and load our hatred on them, how we go to war—and then how later we come to our senses and perceive that ills are not to be so simply projected on an alien group.

Remember?

That is what I don't want to forget.

The Trouble with Reading

When a goat likes a book, the whole book is gone,
and the meaning has to go find an author again.
But when we read, it's just print—deciphering,
like frost on a window: we learn the meaning
but lose what the frost is, and all that world
pressed so desperately behind.

So some time let's discover how the ink
feels, to be clutching all that eternity onto
page after page. But maybe it is better not
to know; ignorance, that wide country,
rewards you just to accept it. You plunge;
it holds you. And you have become a rich darkness.

From *Passwords* (New York: HarperCollins, 1991).

The Farm on the Great Plains

A telephone line goes cold;
birds tread it wherever it goes.
A farm back of a great plain
tugs an end of the line.

I call that farm every year,
ringing it, listening, still;
no one is home at the farm,
the line gives only a hum.

Some year I will ring the line
on a night at last the right one,
and with an eye tapered for braille
from the phone on the wall

I will see the tenant who waits—
the last one left at the place;
through the dark my braille eye
will lovingly touch his face.

"Hello, is Mother at home?"
No one is home today.
"But Father—he should be there."
No one—no one is here.

"But you—are you the one. . . ?"
Then the line will be gone
because both ends will be home:
no space, no birds, no farm.

From Paul Engle and Joseph Langland, eds., *Poet's Choice* (New York: Dial Press, 1962).

My self will be the plain,
wise as winter is gray,
pure as cold posts go
pacing toward what I know.

A glance at "The Farm on the Great Plains" jolts me with a succession of regrets about it, but these regrets link with reassurances as I confront and accept something of my portion in writing: an appearance of moral commitment mixed with a deliberate—even a flaunted—nonsophistication; an organized form cavalierly treated; a trace of narrative for company amid too many feelings. There are emergences of consciousness in the poem, and some outlandish lunges for communication; but I can stand quite a bit of this sort of thing if a total poem gives evidence of locating itself.

And the *things* here—plains, farm, home, winter, lavished all over the page—these command my allegiance in a way that is beyond my power to analyze at the moment. Might I hazard that they signal something like austere hope? At any rate, they possess me. I continue to be a willing participant in the feelings and contradictions that led me to write the poem.

Fifteen

South of the bridge on Seventeenth
I found back of the willows one summer
day a motorcycle with engine running
as it lay on its side, ticking over
slowly in the high grass. I was fifteen.

I admired all that pulsing gleam, the
shiny flanks, the demure headlights
fringed where it lay; I led it gently
to the road and stood with that
companion, ready and friendly. I was fifteen.

We could find the end of a road, meet
the sky on out Seventeenth. I thought about
hills, and patting the handle got back a
confident opinion. On the bridge we indulged
a forward feeling, a tremble. I was fifteen.

Thinking, back farther in the grass I found
the owner, just coming to, where he had flipped
over the rail. He had blood on his hand, was pale—
I helped him walk to his machine. He ran his hand
over it, called me good man, roared away.

I stood there, fifteen.

Whatever its effect on others, several elements do please me in
this little descriptive account of a boy finding a motorcycle. As

Poem and commentary from "Poems for Young Readers," 56th annual
NCTE convention, November 24–26, 1966.

the story first began to spin itself out in the writing, its ingredients fell into two patterns at once: they were conducting themselves as a recounting of an experience, and they were building up a cumulative implication. A boy, fifteen, exploring toward Seventeenth, stumbles upon a gleaming, enticing object ordinarily out of his reach; and in the natural encounter with this new object he endures several immediate, vivid intimations which both entice and disturb him. The machine comes to life as a demure, friendly, ready companion; and as the two beings face ahead, their road meets the sky. But their encounter comes down to earth when the older person, who owns the machine, repossesses it. He is confident, and with a bloody hand he calmly takes over, and roars away.

Another aspect of the account is its form. As the successive parts unfolded themselves for me they lent themselves naturally to a functional and almost inevitable refrain: fifteen. The word takes on useful incremental meaning to culminate at the end: a form finds itself. Other sounds, too, chime along throughout the lines. But of course I should not gloat over the scattered effects which first enticed me along in the writing. Don't you agree that the poem ticks along there and has some latent power too? Or so I feel as I riffle it with my inky hand, while I sit here, fifty-two.

Traveling through the Dark

Traveling through the dark I found a deer
dead on the edge of the Wilson River road.
It is usually best to roll them into the canyon:
that road is narrow; to swerve might make more dead.

By glow of the tail-light I stumbled back of the car
and stood by the heap, a doe, a recent killing;
she had stiffened already, almost cold.
I dragged her off; she was large in the belly.

My fingers touching her side brought me the reason—
her side was warm; her fawn lay there waiting,
alive, still, never to be born.
Beside that mountain road I hesitated.

The car aimed ahead its lowered parking lights;
under the hood purred the steady engine.
I stood in the glare of the warm exhaust turning red;
around our group I could hear the wilderness listen.

I thought hard for us all—my only swerving—,
then pushed her over the edge into the river.

Wednesday nights, late, I drive seventy-five miles home over the Coast Range, after teaching an evening class in Tillamook. Thursday mornings at breakfast my children—Bret, Kim, Kit, Barbara—ask, "What did you see last night, Daddy?" And one Thursday morning I found myself telling them an incident, just

From Warren Carrier and Paul Engle, eds., *Reading Modern Poetry: A Critical Anthology* (New York: Scott, Foresman, 1968).

a routine event on that narrow mountain road. Amid the story, while they listened wide-eyed to Daddy's far, late adventure, I realized that the world had offered to me again an event which could not be held small: a quick wash of feeling signaled for the children and for me that a poem or story had happened, regardless of whether we wrote it down or called it so. Like Cassandra, we felt the past and the future come to bear on the present, and with that triple weight of realization the creative event had occurred, in a flash, without management, just from helpless participation and then willed assent, as often before: an experience unfolds the depth any experience may conceal till it is touched and sprung into its poem or story.

For nothing in life exists without implications, potentials. To live is to traverse landscapes with connotations, to meet people and things with millions of relatives, to find yourself reacting to anything new with all the weight of your past crystalizing into what is before you. In a sense, any account you make becomes a documentary in which you cannot write or tell fast enough to find your way out of the story you carry along. My story that Thursday morning carried in it a multitude of influences which hovered and cried for engagement.

Watching the children, I saw the account reflected, and saw it come to life. The language cocked their attention—that animal so poignantly named, a deer; the dark night, the wild mountains, the narrow road, the sound of rushing water; and then— our faithful automobile. And standing in that emergency, far from their sleeping selves—their father, at a loss, confronting a framed, stopped, meaningful picture. With a jolt we felt the usually disguised imminence of first and last things.

It would be possible to trace the decisions in the writing of this already formed poem—the lines, the insistent part-rhymes. There were decisions forced on the writer, inherent in the meaning, such as the need for absolute confrontations early—"dead," "killing," "stiffened," "cold"—as a firm assertion of what must be faced without swerving at the end. There were discoveries, for instance that the taillight makes a red cloud in the cold night as the steady exhaust signals readiness. There are a host of participating details begging to enter the poem, but there is also the hesitant writer and doer of the action, afraid to blur what he glimpsed, awkwardly selecting one part at a time and counting on the hearer to participate where distractions might threaten whatever potential there is in the minimum telling.

Once a poem like this is started, there are many ways to intensify; and there are a myriad of nuances to be accepted by the writer or to be sacrificed. But what looms in such a documentary is that the main effect depends on concurrence of event and implications. Writing the poem becomes a process of discovering what elements contribute adequately to the distinction of the event—this time such elements as the lone traveling, the darkness, the soft animal, the road that led onward. My mission as poet was simply to tell others how it was to travel that road: in their learning about my experience they would be reading back from the event into the many aspects of their own experience which were shadowed forth by the very simplicity of my encounter. Almost any reaction I had—in a local, physical way—to the experience with the deer would deliver for the reader something of the loneliness and the minimum scope for action we all have in extreme situations.

Two other considerations deserve emphasis in accounting for this poem. The first is that telling it consisted from the first in simply delivering how it was to stand there in the dark with the deer; not till the account took shape did I become aware of patterns which could be identified as symbolic. My first impulse was toward narrative: once I saw the parallels looming along that narrative thread, I did not deny nor try to avoid them, but my only guide in the telling was to grope for *how it was*. The other consideration is about form, and in a sense about wording—about intensifying the verbal voltage of the poem: much of the syllable-help, the sound-reinforcement, arrives with the thought in the telling; but any regularizing of the pattern (second and fourth lines with near rhyme, for instance) comes from a find of nondesperate, even confident juggling. All such decisions offer themselves to the writer, and he can welcome gains and give up certain sacrifices with an almost relaxed feeling of consideration—a process different from the more adventurous and hazardous feel of the first telling, the discovery of the main narrative.

This kind of poem is a sure kind. It may not be spectacular, but it can always possess the validity of reporting something. It can be intensified in the writing, but its most significant value derives from the relevance and the pervasiveness of it as a metaphor. If it catches many experiences in its pattern, it can be very powerful. One may be struck at any time by this kind of ghostly accompaniment, the symbolic reinforcing inherent in the way we have to think, and inherent in the language our past offers us when we use it for today's purposes.

Even after telling the story of traveling through the dark I cannot rid myself of its hold over me, nor could I that Thursday morning, as I pushed the children—Bret, Kim, Kit, Barbara—out on their road to school, and then went on my own way to work, where I had to be, ready for the next encounter, the next poem, and so on. . . .

Stereopticon

This can happen. They can bring the leaves back
to the cottonwood trees, those great big rooms
where our street—as long as summer—led
to the river. From a rusty nail in the alley
someone can die, but the street go on again.

Hitler and others, those pipsqueak voices,
can twitter from speakers. I can look back
from hills beyond town, and every person
and all the alleys, and even the buildings
except the church be hidden in leaves.

This can happen, my parents laughing
because they have already won. And I can
study and grow up and look back and call "Wait!"
and run after their old green car
and be lost again.

When I look back at a poem of mine I may shake my head, but it is a friendly shake. So it is when I look at "Stereopticon." Many elements from my life are here: little towns, vacation time, the kids on the block entering their own big, tall-tree world of climbing and ranging down to the river—and stepping on rusty nails.

And here comes history—mine was the generation that encountered the upsets of World War II. We were taken from home—it all disappeared (except maybe the tallest things, like the church steeple). My poem starts early and near; it ranges

Commentary unpublished, n.d. Poem from *Writing the Australian Crawl* (Ann Arbor: University of Michigan Press, 1978).

into the big world; and it even becomes philosophical (but in specific terms) at the end. Yes, I feel friendly about it. Though I did not write it in order to match any patterns or archetypes, I see now that its parts have a firm place in a human pattern we all share; writing my poem has taken the pieces natural to my own life and fitted them, without any forcing on my part, into something negotiable, a poem that links outward. I am not surprised, but it takes the intention to analyze my own poem to bring me to see its universality. I write from my immediate feelings; something bigger than myself has included me.

If I look at how the language forwards itself in the poem, I am again surprised and confirmed. Roving up and down the lines, I come upon lingering sequences of sound; they are scattered, not formally present like rhymes at the ends of lines. And my cadences move forward, twisting and dancing. I feel pity for those formalists who have to count measures or match a standard "form"! If I let myself concur with the me that blundered along through the writing, I see reinforcements offered me by the language—bonuses found during the writing, opportunities too rich and unorthodox to be anticipated. I am confirmed in my belief that the way to write is to go forward optimistically, allowing the encounters of Now to be the guides onward.

What bonuses? Well, if poetry gains from repetition, might I welcome whole clusters of repetition in the first line?—"This can happen. They can bring . . ." I coast downward and find linked-forward cousin sounds: leaves-river-Hitler-twitter. I find strange patterns no one has put a name to (I guess): every person . . . all the alleys . . . even the building. . . . I feel a drift, a helpful drift, in the language.

I didn't find patterns from preexisting intentions; I let the experience of writing the poem bring me many, many options. And some of them I took.

Then when I draw backward and look at the title, and the happen-happen-run-again-again thread through the poem, I shake my head: good? Oh, maybe, maybe not. Me? Yes. Do I mean it? Yes. A poem? In my terms, yes. A reader is invited to look with a special kind of attention at a sequence that reinforces itself; time is redeemed by art—or luck. I hunt for that kind of luck.

Ask Me

Some time when the river is ice ask me
mistakes I have made. Ask me whether
what I have done is my life. Others
have come in their slow way into
my thought, and some have tried to help
or to hurt: ask me what difference
their strongest love or hate has made.

I will listen to what you say.
You and I can turn and look
at the silent river and wait. We know
the current is there, hidden; and there
are comings and goings from miles away
that hold the stillness exactly before us.
What the river says, that is what I say.

My poem started from amid random writing I was doing in my usual morning attempts to scare up something by putting anything down that came to mind. I was at a country place; it was early morning; I was all alone, and feeling that way—in a pleasant way, with a fire in the Franklin stove, the dark outside. It was winter, and I guess the cold made me launch in the way I did, "Some time when the river is ice . . ."

This poem stayed in much its original order—more so than most of mine. Writing it was like getting a lock on a feeling and just letting the feeling lead me from one part to the next. This is

From Albert Turner, ed., *Fifty Contemporary Poets: The Creative Process* (New York: Longman, 1977).

not to say that the elements mentioned stayed the same, but the changes themselves (the changes of topic, I mean) were just a following of the feeling.

My impulse is to say that I had no principles of technique at all in mind. As I look back over the first draft, I do realize, though, that I was getting satisfaction out of syncopating along in the sentences; that is, I find some pleasure in just opening and closing sentences—starting and then holding before myself a feeling that the measure and flow of utterance will lend itself to an easy forwarding of what I am saying. I guess I am trying to own up to a pervasive *security* in language, but the feeling is not consciously based on use of a technique in any sense I have known others to define it.

As in almost all of my writing, I was not aiming toward any reader: my entry into the process was through inward satisfactions I felt as the language led me onward. If I quiz myself now, I am able to assume that I was *accompanied by* a sense of being able to tell someone, sometime, something like what I was putting down; that person would not necessarily be congenial—maybe someone I was going to *tell off*. But that person would also be participating in the steady unfolding of what was said.

I think my poem can be paraphrased—and that any poem can be paraphrased. But every pass through the material, using other words, would have to be achieved at certain costs, either in momentum, or nuance, or dangerously explicit (and therefore misleading in tone) adjustments. I'll try one such pass through the poem:

> When it's quiet and cold and we have some chance to
> interchange without hurry, confront me if you like with a
> challenge about whether I think I have made mistakes in
> my life—and ask me, if you want to, whether to me my life
> is actually the sequence of events or exploits others would
> see. Well, those others tag along in my living, and some of
> them in fact have played significant roles in the narrative
> run of my world; they have intended either helping or
> hurting (but by implication in the way I am saying this you
> will know that neither effort is conclusive). So—ask me
> how important their good or bad intentions have been (both
> intentions get a drastic *leveling* judgment from this cool

stating of it all). You, too, will be entering that realm of
maybe-help-maybe-hurt, by entering that far into my life by
asking this serious question—so: I will stay still and
consider. Out there will be the world confronting us both;
we will both know we are surrounded by mystery,
tremendous things that do not reveal themselves to us. That
river, that world—and our lives—all share the depth and
stillness of much more significance than our talk, or
intentions. There is a steadiness and somehow a solace in
knowing that what is around us so greatly surpasses
our human concerns.

This poem shares with many of my poems a tone of accepting
what comes. Human affairs get perspective by affairs other
than human. This poem is much more serious, unrelenting,
than most—but not all—of my other poems. It is *one of the ways*
that occur to me. It is like almost all of my other poems, though,
in a deep way—it comes about through willing entry into what-
ever mood or whatever opportunities a time and place and the
chances of language offer me.

This poem, like almost all my poems, came from free associa-
tion, that is, free allowing of my impulses to find their immedi-
ate interest. I was aware of a steady forward cadence. This poem
went through only about three complete drafts, and the first
writing of the poem was much more clear and *set* than most; the
changes were a teasing out of opportunities perceived in the
first draft. And I believe the poem was essentially complete
within three days (and I was of course not on it all that time).
The structure, theme, and tone just kept on being what they
started out to be—working on the poem was like telling it—"go
ahead, be yourself." My lines are generally just about equal;
where a line breaks, though, means something to me, and some
of the juggling was meant to preserve how definite the slash line
is in such changeover sequences as me/mistakes, have/done,
and/some, etc. I was aware of *current is there . . . there are*, things
like that—willingnesses to repeat, coasting the sounds. . . .

I would like my poem to be read aloud in a serious voice
without any relenting, but silent reading by a person feeling it
would be all right.

I did not consider metaphor at all. I know—and I suppose at the time I knew with an immediacy and a gusto—that "river is ice" for instance can't just be present without an effect; but in writing I found my way forward to accepting the feelings and saying what occurred to me—metaphorical elements sweep into the utterance, but not by intent. In some ways, I now see, I was putting the reader into stern obligation to accept a forceful metaphor but without my revealing by any tremor that the metaphorical elements were anything other than *necessary* parts of what I was saying.

I ordinarily feel that I am not using abstract language; I am afraid to solicit the reader's or hearer's feelings—I yearn to hand him or her a situation or scene that will coerce human involvement, not request it.

One mannerism, I now see, is that this whole poem addresses another person as if present; the poem maneuvers another person into being the one who demands the account given. I believe I was sliding away from that kind of poem that proclaims—I was indulging a prevalent yen of mine—to keep away from the appearance of elbowing in.

I was using the tug of narrative, a thing I like to do. And I was avoiding anything high at the end. The persona is a part of myself—one of my ways (at least in fancy)—understanding but grabbing. I was not jumpy about cliché—I usually like to be pretty close, as if willing to say any dumb thing (with a nudge that keeps it from quite that—I hope).

The poem is a lump—the reader is in for a block of something—"shape" on the page.

I assume that any human being, with the right context, would respond to the surface of this poem. I believe some would assume that it did not make enough claims. That conviction on their part would be a measure of their smugness or craving for sweets, and even they might have a faint hint of missing something.

Reaching into the Well

Kierkegaard said, "Drink from your own well." And I like that, taking it to mean that each of us has an individual source for our best work, and that to reach deliberately elsewhere is to neglect something essential in our writing.

So when I get up in the morning and settle down to write, I do not reach for what is timely or in style, but for something that suggests itself to me right at the moment. It can be any trivial word or even syllable, or a sound from the trees outside, or what day it is, or that the sun is about to come up—anything. And sometimes I feel that the more trivial it seems the better, for with nothing to live up to I can relax and catch onto a current within me.

Yesterday, for instance, crows were raising a ruckus in the big fir trees across the street. For some reason great flocks like to circle around up there, at their own level, getting ready for some really important events. So I began to jot down rambling ideas. I remembered how crows will get excited about an owl. I put that down and worried it around awhile, but it wasn't getting anywhere.

Then, out of nowhere, I got a feeling, a lonely, dark feeling. What great looming eventualities lurked out there in the dark? It is a silence; it hovers beyond the crows, beyond any sound. Our daily excitements take place before that backdrop. And I doodled around with that idea.

Two other significant—to me—things happened in that spell of writing. One was that a title occurred to me, a kind of ambi-

---

Commentary unpublished, n.d. "Why the Sun Comes Up," from *The Long Sigh the Wind Makes* (Monmouth, OR: Adrienne Lee Press, 1991).

tious but at the same time offhand title, just the kind that appealed at the time.

And the other was that again on this aimless morning I had found my way into what struck me as my own typical well—a brash story that included a glimpse into darkness and then affirmed the light.

Here is what I made of that session, maybe a poem, maybe just another foray into the limitless possibilities for what writing can bring me. But in any event an OK bit of jotting for which I was thankful. It might lead somewhere, in itself, or when I again settle down to write:

Why the Sun Comes Up

To be ready again if they find an owl, crows
choose any old tree before dawn and hold a convention
where they practice their outrage routine. "Let's elect
someone." "No, no! Forget it." They
see how many crows can dance on a limb.
"Hey, listen to this one." One old crow
flaps away off and looks toward the east. In that
lonely blackness God begins to speak
in a silence beyond all that moves. Delighted
wings move close and almost touch each other.
Everything stops for a minute, and the sun rises.

The Writing of "Bess"

Ours are the streets where Bess first met her
cancer. She went to work every day past the
secure houses. At her job in the library
she arranged better and better flowers, and when
students asked for books her hand went out
to help. In the last year of her life
she had to keep her friends from knowing
how happy they were. She listened while they
complained about food or work or the weather.
And the great national events danced
their grotesque, fake importance. Always

Pain moved where she moved. She walked
ahead; it came. She hid; it found her.
No one ever served another so truly;
no enemy ever meant so strong a hate.
It was almost as if there was no room
left for her on earth. But she remembered
where joy used to live. She straightened its flowers;
she did not weep when she passed its houses;
and when finally she pulled into a tiny corner
and slipped from pain, her hand opened
again, and the streets opened, and she wished all well.

In a quiet town of ordinary people and events, and without any
fanfare or warning, an absolute, individual event occurs. It is a
thing that can happen to anyone, quietly. Its name immediately

---

From *Writer's Digest,* February 1992.

establishes its power and menace. It is an easy word, universally recognized: cancer.

That term appears once in my poem "Bess," as the last word in the first sentence. The sentence is straightforward, all monosyllables except that name. And the name manages to show up isolated, after the first line-break, calmly present and alone.

Further, the name ends with a growl sound: *er*. That sound announces itself six previous times in the sentence, stealthily dropping its hints of threat. A reader could go through the whole poem and wonder if the writer ever uses form—rhyme, for instance. And that same reader would have been influenced by rhyme seven times in the first sentence.

On that subject, let me pause for a minute to consider sound. For me, all sounds rhyme, sort of. Coming out of silence, a voice begins its roving among utterances. There is always a continuity, a modulation that hints at similarities both close and distant. Rather than being occasionally or regularly engaged with identifiable repetitions in sound, a poet is constantly caught up in waves of mutually influencing syllables. That music can be assertive, or it can be elusive. But it is always present. And in its more elusive ways it can shimmer line after line.

When my wife told of a dear friend, a librarian at her school, just diagnosed with cancer, this poem began in my journal with the phrase *These are the streets . . .* Later in revision the line became *Ours are the streets*, as the somber tone of the poem began to assert itself.

That somber tone, however, must be muted in the lines that follow; for this whole poem will become a holding off of sorrow. Bess will walk our secure streets. In her work she will touch flowers, help children; her hand—that hand with its ultimate task in the last line of the poem—will have a life of its own, will go out to help.

Apart from any sound or rhythm tactics employed, this poem's relentless task—in its first half, its first stanza—is to hold off that somber note struck in the first sentence. Within the terrible room she has been assigned to, Bess will come to see her friends' lives in a new way. Their troubles take on an aspect so trivial that Bess can't bear to let them know what she sees.

And the "world" events also turn into pitiful fictions; the

concerns of other people, the important topics of the day—these are abruptly reduced so drastically that Bess can't bear to let others know what they are doing. Part of her work becomes enduring the loneliness of one who knows.

And then in a single, isolated word that reaches over to end the first stanza by beginning the second, the inner travail of Bess begins: *Always* . . .

And the second half of the poem takes up its key word: *Pain.* Again the stanza begins with a line of monosyllables, except for the last word, which—as in the first stanza—comes at the beginning of the second line. And the pattern is *moved . . . moved . . . walked ahead.* There is no place on earth for Bess; her enemy seeks her out. Her town, her job, the houses of her friends—these are reduced to the background for something that she carries all alone. The poem should accompany her, stay direct, stay in key with its beginning stanza—and begin the coasting-to-an-end trajectory that such an experience as this poem has to follow.

And that unwinding, lowered-wings course toward the end gives me a chance to use one of the standard moves in a poem, the recapitulation of elements that were established in the first stanza: Bess remembers joy, straightens its flowers, walks ahead past her friends' houses without burdening them with her tragedy.

And the hand which had helped is able to open in offering once more. Steady in the face of death and pain, Bess hands a wish to those around her. And her poem, never making much of its music, finally allows itself to remark with a tolling, chiming sound in the last two words, *all well.*

Whatever its cadences, whatever its alternations of long and short phrasings, and whatever final assessment made about it, this poem, it seems to me, stays in focus. The language does, as it must, stay in key with the life of Bess, unassuming, but straight on. Significant without claiming to be so. The writing of it, as is always the case when the words are right, gave me contexts for saying things I have always wanted to say, or at least been ready to say when given occasion to recognize my need. That is one of the great rewards of discovering a poem as you write it: attitudes central to your life find their way into what emerges on the page.

But those emergences have to inhabit the tangible surrounding world: residues of the circumstances behind this poem lurk throughout its lines. I am glad to welcome such local connections, both when I originally write and in the work's final form; often such chance connections seem to me helpful, authenticating, just rough enough to give life to a finished poem.

For instance the title is simply the name of our friend who experienced that *last year of her life.* Her plain, familiar name is forever linked to our memories of her. She was the librarian in the grade school beside our house, the school where my wife taught. Her streets were our streets; her life—and death—touched us. What my surroundings offer I tend to accept into my writings, with changes only for reasons that press themselves on me as the work develops.

And with a twist of recognition I can see some of my own familiar *inner* streets crowding into this poem: in the form of the belittling reference to *the great national events,* or the glance at the triviality of many people's complaints (food, work, weather). I live by these crochets of mine and they insinuate my points of view into whatever I write.

Even one of my daily pleasures in writing—the playing of sentences like an accordion—short, staccato utterances countering stretched-out lengths of lingo—I see and welcome in the conclusion of this poem. *She walked ahead; it came. She hid; it found her*—and then, and then, longer and longer it goes, from two-word clauses at the beginning to a five-line sentence at the end. For me this is all part of the trajectory a poem finds its way to having.

And only after undertaking the awkward task of considering my own poem do I recognize some further enticements in it for me, as writer. It has a riveted coherence, without relying on extra words to help hold it together: one person, one event, one inevitable finish. It concerns not so much my choice of words, but rather my not having to make many choices—that feels good to me.

Like a lifeline through the poem recur the actions of Bess: Bess met, she went, she arranged, she listened, she moved, she walked, she hid, she remembered, she straightened, she did not weep, she passed, she pulled, she wished. And by the simplest of coherence devices—a pronoun—the rest of the poem completes the course of its unfolding: her job, her hand, her life, her friends . . . and then, again her hand.

How could my job as writer be any easier?

Let me put it this way: if not forced by considerations of nuance and meaning, I do not seek variety. Stay with the core of your poem, I say. Smart is OK, but lucky is better. Find the language that leads you easily onward in so natural a way that you do not have to be smart.

The needs of the developing poem will suggest what words fit right, and those phrases that emerge will enhance, or *can* enhance, any shabby beginning you had the nerve to start with.

Bess opened her hand for me. In unfolding her story, I let her quality reach out.

Sometimes, Reading

There's a hollow place.
Late at night you can think of it.
And way off beyond it in the dark someone is laughing.

That person laughing is a writer named Nietzsche.
A doubt begins to grow in your mind:
his books hover in space winking on and off, up, down.

You come back from the book you are reading.
It is now again and the world has come back.
But it feels different. Never the same.

That one time, reading, it was in the browsing room at the University of Kansas, just before World War II. I happened to reach for a text, *The Birth of Tragedy*. An hour later when I looked up—a changed world, deeper but full of wonder and excitement, not to be trusted, but infinitely ready for revelation. Why hadn't my professors told me about this new hemisphere? They had cheated me. Or didn't they know about it?

Sure, I had read before, the family evenings, the library at Liberal during high school; my world was full of books, Kipling (my father's favorite, "Now the four-way lodge is open, now the hunting winds are loosed . . ."), Willa Cather (my mother's life in the early days on the plains, *A Lantern in Her Hand*), Edgar Lee Masters ("Out of me unworthy and unknown . . . ," "It takes life to love life . . ."), the contests to read the current favorite around the dining table ("Hats off, along the street there comes the blare of bugles the ruffle of drums . . .").

From *Ohio Review*, fall 1993.

Sure, I was a reader. But this—this Nietzsche, these blazes of outrageous but tantalizing discovery: "Every word is a prejudice"; "The best way through the mountains is from peak to peak, but it takes long legs"; "The right eye shouldn't trust the left."

> The world turned over. It began to
> come apart. What held it together
> through all those years of my childhood
> separated into hundreds of little pieces—
> parents who loved me, my country 'tis,
> libraries with shelves full of truth,
> Santa Claus. I couldn't hold on any more.

But a new expanse became mine, wild, reckless (so reckless it could be conservative too), a rampage of gusto: Galileo (thought experiments), John Henry Newman (two and two only self-evident beings, myself and my creator), Pascal (the awful silence of those infinite spaces), Kierkegaard (drink from your own well, purity of heart is to will one thing), George Eliot (in death they were not divided), Tolstoy, Gandhi, Saint Teresa (let mine eyes see thee, sweet Jesus of Nazareth), Goethe (man is a creature for a limited condition), Wittgenstein (we must unlearn what educated people know). . . . These names and immediate forays into their books throng to mind; and the spaciousness of it all I link to that evening in the browsing room.

And in my writing, I feel the presence of that new continent, an influence more pervasive and important than any consideration of writing craft: "Traveling through the dark I found a deer . . . ," "In the late night listening from bed I have joined the ambulance or the patrol . . . ," "Ask me mistakes I have made . . ." These glimpses, to me, have the flavor of that new world.

Reading now, I stop and remember the KU library, evening coming on, the shadows, the students bent over books (but only on their side of Nietzsche), and my world now reels on, the world of literature, of superfact. But OK, big and scary as it is.

It feels OK.

Cross my heart.

III
The Art of Teaching

Eighth-Grade Art

Certain people gave off an electric field. Near them, your hair stood up. All day their bodies lived cooped in the little cage of their clothes, and if you touched them they would fly away.

The new teacher was like that. I sat near her desk and watched while she slowly lifted up a bright painting of horses alive and prancing—"*The Horse Fair,* by Rosa Bonheur," she said. I would never forget. "*The Angelus,*" she said. I looked at the bowed heads, the dark world around them. A strong feeling of goodness flooded my mind. The teacher leaned forward; she tenderly looked at the class.

Some people, maybe treated coldly when young, turn hard and selfish, to survive. But they also may need someone soft as a teddy bear, for a companion.

On the way home from school, the forgiving trees, Norway maple and elm, leaned over me, holding out new branches for a little light, a little rain. All they need, really, is time—the rest they can work out, waiting in a bad year, getting generous when any invitation from the air even hints at being friendly. They wait for an invitation, and God reaches for them sometimes, on a stormy night. They were waiting, just like *The Angelus,* or sometimes like *The Horse Fair.*

At home I told my mother about Rosa Bonheur and about the pictures. "Do you think you will be an artist?" she asked. And I said maybe.

"Did you like the teacher?"

"Yes."

From *Hungry Mind Review* 15 (fall 1990).

Teaching Notes

Produce, Reflect, Perceive

Students' reactions to each other are creative, public and revealing.

ð❧

An art teacher is not a standards person.

ð❧

We are all exactly equal (your critics too). In a workshop there are no bad (or good) poems.

ð❧

My whole intent is to give allegiance at once to each student; each one has hired me, and my job is to be available, but never to intrude. This readiness intends to establish trust, a non-judgmental atmosphere in the class.

ð❧

All assessment is a hazard to learning, by subtly changing the inner guidance of the activity to an organizing for outer rewards.

ð❧

One way to induce writing without assessment is to have a poetry wall.

ð❧

From "Notes for Arts Propel," unpublished, n.d.

My ambition is to be delicate as a seismograph. Students are going to meet intellectual Tai Chi. And after a first shock and disbelief, they are going to love it: they have a friend who will listen and react, but neither praise nor blame. It's new. It hands them real control.

§

Yes, we can assess art. The *doing* of art, though, requires—paradoxically—a recklessness.

§

Writing is more than "recording ideas." Writing is creative.

§

Harness all the sled dogs.

§

People are more than their current selves. Art derives from weaknesses as well as strengths.

§

We do not "correct" a piece of writing; we question a life.

Sharing Language

A Conversation with David L. Elliott

For some people you're one of the patron saints of process writing in composition classes, with regard to techniques for prewriting.

All right!

In articles and textbooks, I've seen quotes from you about following whatever happens to come along in the writing process. And that's something we try to help our students with the most, to help them overcome writing blocks and the feeling that they can't get it out. People have found some of the things you say very useful because so often these days in teaching freshman composition we get students who just can't write. I don't mean not knowing the grammar, although that's certainly part of it. Are you aware of what I'm saying, that people claim you as an authority in composition classes? On the other hand, sometimes people say, "Isn't he primarily talking about writing poetry, or is he talking about something that would be true for freshman English with absolute beginners?"

Everything. Now let me try to link together two things you said. You are too doctrinaire about people who can't write. Sure, everybody can write. I'm manifesting now what this is about: you just lower your standards and start there. So when I'm teaching any group I naturally don't—but also by principle I

From David L. Elliott, "Sharing Language," *Teaching English in the Two-Year College,* December 1991. Copyright 1991 by the National Council of Teachers of English. Reprinted with permission.

don't—have standards. I am not disappointed in what someone says or writes because I'm not expecting anything except what comes. I'm just there, wherever it is. Sea level is where it is in this class, that's all. So, it's something I find in a class rather than having my idea of where it ought to be when I go in there; I just find it. That's part of it. I'll just make that little excursion.

Then to go back to what you said about being the patron saint or something of this process. I have, and I welcome in myself, just a childlike delight in what you say. I'm very glad to hear that, and I don't want to claim anything, but I will say—and I have said it when it was hard to say it, when I didn't do myself any good—I'll take my stand by that way of writing and teaching writing. Where it all came from I don't know. I mean it may have had another source, but it also sprang up wherever I was. It was just something that began to be *the way it is* for me, and I'm delighted to find (whoever the saint is) this process, or the recognition of making progress and doing art by acceptance and convergence—all these things. It's where I live.

I probably was too doctrinaire in saying that about students who can't write, but in a sense I was quoting what the students would say about themselves: "I can't write."

I know they would. I wouldn't accept that.

I think your ideas help them cope with the feeling that they are tongue-tied, pen-tied, whatever you want to call it. I want to say to them, "Get it out; don't worry about it." But it took a long time before a number of composition teachers were able to accept that idea. It seemed too loose, too easy somehow.

Maybe it is safer for me if I back up for a minute and say there are many people going around the country now with this process, exemplifying it. My hat is off to them, and when I meet them I feel convergent with them. Nobody is making any claims, but I just feel wholehearted allegiance. There are quite a number of them.

I was talking only a couple of days ago with people who were saying, "They've got to know the grammar before they can write." But if they are never going to write, what good is the grammar?

Well, the awful thing is they know it. I mean grammar is what people use when they talk. I saw it defined a long time ago as the unconscious logic of the popular mind. To assume that mastery of punctuation, spelling, and how to avoid the more obvious of society's no-no's about the form of discourse will release students for a life of perfect talking and writing is nonsense, and dangerous nonsense. We have enough correct fools.

I have heard you say that you don't want to praise your students' writing. You don't want to disparage, but you don't want to praise either. But I often find myself dealing with students whose sense of written language is almost nonexistent. They really don't have any models that they have processed and which have become voices in their head that they can compare their writings to or get a sense of inspiration from. They are more an oral culture, and writing is something that has just not played much of a role in their lives. So when they make their achievements in writing, when they begin to do it, I always feel I want to encourage that along. But you have made me think twice. How would you deal with such students?

Well, I feel easy about asserting something here. I don't want to push it; I want to put some "maybe" into this. But it seems easy to me in the real world to meet any student, no matter how afraid they are of writing, and if they write anything down, I would look at what they have done as evidence (I don't know a better way to say this)—not as composition but as evidence of something that is happening with them and the language. And I would not pat them on the head for this to encourage them (and if I could control my inner feelings, I would, and I think I can because I'm wholehearted about this) but I would respond to it. I mean I would indicate where I converged with what they had written: and maybe any remarks, either written or spoken, in the presence of what they have written, would be like "Kilroy was here" remarks to indicate that I was with them at this point, that I was following it. I mean I'm enigmatic about evaluation, just saying, "I was at that same corner that you're talking about," or "That's the building that such and such happened in." It indicates, "Yes, he did read it, but he didn't say good or bad." Sometimes I am not able to follow it, in which case I wouldn't hesitate to tell them I was not able to follow it. But I wouldn't ever try to tell them I couldn't follow it when I really could. And it's got to be really low if I can't understand it. I tell them things like "I can understand the Rosetta Stone, no problem."

So, I think any student, any person talking or writing, is better served by attention and listening, reading and accompanying that person, than by being the machine in their presence who says "good" or "bad." I'm a human being. Is any person's writing utterly foreign to me? No, I've been there before, you know. It's not exactly understanding. It's not exactly trying to empathize, but it is sharing the experience of language.

I've never found anyone in actual life whose writing was just gibberish. You know, you said and we all say things like this— they really can't write well. If they come to college, they can probably draw out some words. They can draw out these words, and it's some words and not other words, and so I just begin to go into what words they are and what other words they aren't rather than encouraging them by saying "good." In some ways it's as easy as this: just be honest. My kind of honesty . . . I mean there is no problem for me, since I'm not expecting anything—I just have hopes. You could even indicate that to them and it wouldn't hurt them because they have already made that judgment that it's no good. So I don't disagree with them; I mean if they say it's no good, I see *how* it's no good, or something like that. Why did this go this way? Rather than "no" or "yes," it is "where?" "tell me more," "help me."

Maybe I can get the stance to take by citing this. A person told me years ago, "I talked to an editor and I said, 'When you get something that is really no good, what do you do?' This editor said, 'I ask myself what it is in me that is keeping me from perceiving what is in this particular work.' " I think that would be a helpful attitude to take. So, you see, there is evidence. I feel like a kind of super-Freud: "Does this have meaning?" Oh yes. More than you thought.

But you were saying that when a student comes up to you and says, "Should I do it this way or this way?" you are very forthright in giving advice.

I am forthright because then I know that we have converged where they are. They're ready for one or the other and they are really asking me something, which would not be demeaning of me. I would not demean them and I wouldn't assume any ignorance; I would just tell them what I feel. That's a wonderful place to be, and if they can get the feel of that for themselves, they shouldn't try to do any more than that. That's all there is in writing—this way or this way, rather than good or bad because good may be impossible, and bad is somebody else's judgment; it just happens to be where you are. So why not "this way or this way"?

Could you say more about how students are harmed by evaluation and why they do not benefit from praise?

If a student learns to seek praise and avoid blame, the actual feel and excitement of learning and accomplishing will be slighted in favor of someone else's reaction. The student's own, inner, self-realizing relation to the materials is displaced. Anyone who customarily seeks outside rewards rather than inner satisfactions will be disabled, it seems to me, for all higher and original accomplishment. And that kind of teaching and "learning" will corrupt both student and teacher. For teachers will begin to feel themselves arbiters and guardians rather than participants in the excitement of skill and discovery.

How do you cope with the demand for evaluation placed upon teachers by the educational system, by administrators, or even by students?

Once I took on the participating rather than the judging role, I had to be ready for reactions. And I was not heroic. If a student demands an evaluation, I give it; I cave in. And the same for a parent or administrator: I take whatever demands my bosses make (or change bosses, but that is difficult sometimes). My job, it seems to me, is to make clear what I think ought to be done. I can be overruled, and I don't hold grudges about it. But always I let my preference be known. You might be surprised at how prevalently I was allowed my way. And even knowledge of what I *wanted* to do permeated the classroom: students knew I was on their side, on the side of experimentation, of worthy mistakes, of adventure rather than the trudging down established paths that most systems impose.

And let me put in that this nonevaluation impulse applies maybe with more force for beginners. Many teachers seem to think that students new to an endeavor require closely supervised training rather than the more free activity of those who have benefited from the teacher's guidance. Far from it, I say. If anything, the emphasis should be the other way around: beginners benefit from impulse, excitement, motion, trying out things without the menace of disapproval (or the distraction of imminent gaining of approval). The more advanced the student, the more able to take close, hovering, judgmental interchange.

I assume that there is no ceiling on one's education, that "accomplished" students are exalted only because they and their exalters are limited, that out there in the realm of our mutual seeking we all—students, teachers, and, yes, even our bosses— can continue to learn, without the distraction of pats on the head or raps on the knuckles. Education is too important and exciting to be dominated by thoughts of the hovering red pencil or the happy smiling face pasted in the margin.

You have such faith in people and that anyone can write.

[Laughing] No soul is going to be lost.

This faith that somehow there is that within everyone which can manifest itself in writing and in an authentic way seems to be very comfortable for you. A lot of people would say a leap of faith is needed for that.

It *is* comfortable for me, I think, for a number of reasons. For instance Kierkegaard has this: everybody's equal, not in the Jeffersonian sense, but *equal*, in the face of the magnitude of what we don't know. Human presumption about the more or less is quaint; you know, it's provincial, it's provinciality to make much of that. I wrote an article called "A Priest of the Imagination." I guess it's in *You Must Revise Your Life*. But I wrote it to give at a gathering of English teachers, and in it there is this faith, this idea. You know, I'm a priest of the imagination and when I go to class my job is conducting the inner light of those people to wherever it's going.

. . .

I often feel when I'm writing that I'm just present as the language crystallizes into a new poem, and if that is harmonious with deconstruction I'm ready for that. I had that feeling a long time ago. I could have it in the envious way. You know, "Well, Keats was just lucky; he happened to be there ready when the language was just about to become 'Ode on a Grecian Urn.' " I try to get myself related to language in such a way as to encourage it to become what it's ready to become, and I feel compatible with that in many ways. For instance, I don't have this feeling of controlling the language but of just riding it wherever it's going. It's a social thing. Nobody invented it. Nobody that I'm aware of has real ability to guide it. We're going along with it. I feel that I'm sniffing my way forward into the development of the language.

For Our Esteemed Companions on the Way

A Greeting at a Writer's Conference

You guests in our area, in that book you are about to write save a place for the spirit of our part of the country where we welcome you. Here, you can walk a corridor, as in a museum, with spearheads on one side and bombs and pictures of a Navy blimp on the other—a mere one hundred years between. Here, you can see a photograph of Joe Champion, first White settler, who lived in a hollow tree and ate with a carved horn spoon. The scene, as in a museum, is watched by clear wolf eyes and an owl of snow.

In that book you are about to write you may find a reason for how time goes, for everything in the sky, and let the reader climb by the eyes on that strongest thread in the world as you weave the dark and the cold. Readers on a parallel way will follow your book, the smoke signals, the many little fires, converging. Or say they will follow the channel you discover, that you find by whispering and listening and leaning toward what calls back—your book, your secret channel.

We come together to this place, brought by the ratchet of time, seeing each other here, now, and seeing on toward that new book, the one where the air finds every leaf and feather over forest and water, where every character is alive like a light—like us, here in this place. And in that next book words will crowd together and emerge when the book opens by candlelight, and the words will touch the trees and the leaves will turn

From a talk delivered at the Western Writer's Conference, Portland, Oregon, June 26, 1989.

into fire. Every face will turn into a soul wandering this tabernacle world.

In that book you are about to write, how quiet it is now, how calm and sure. But there, everything lengthens and yearns; interstellar space hovers over those fields. You can reach in; you can change all days that follow, anywhere on earth. Those masters Yeats, Pound, and Eliot saw art as growing from other art, but you are alive: you can change anything. You are travelers in *The Word*, with a commission, a freedom, pilgrims of time; you can listen and speak in the mixed wonder and terror of what is coming toward you, the wonder and terror of being alive.

You guests at this conference, with these fragments from my journal, I greet you and end with some echoes from over the centuries when John Milton defended our books and our next book, and the next. May they be as alive "as those fabulous dragon's teeth," springing up; may they "preserve as in a vial the purest efficacy and extraction of that living intellect" you will bring to their making.

No Praise, No Blame

An Interview with George E. Murphy Jr.

Your address concerning "no praise, no blame," as you put it, and the admittedly casual posture you take in workshops have been the source of much attention here. They have served, it seems to me as almost, well, a challenge to poets running workshops.

I would feel successful as a teacher partly in terms of the amount of activity a class was engaging in—not how brilliantly I could talk or something like that. To me, a successful session is one where everybody gets involved. So, there's *that* part of it.

But, also, it is true that I do a lot of assessing in my own mind when I choose what to read, when I choose what to buy—I'm thinking of books, poetry too. It's not that there aren't any standards in my mind or at least tastes and gusto and lack of gusto. But it's that, in the process of writing, and in the process of teaching writing, assessment is in a decidedly secondary position. That it's intrusion from on high by a teacher, is at least delaying the arrival of the students in that desirable position of doing the judging for themselves. After a product is done, editors decide what to publish. I decide what to buy or read or check out of the library. I do all of that. It's just that I separate it from my practice as a writer and a teacher.

Is that to say that assessments, corrections, judgments are editorial functions and not educational functions?

From *Small Farm* 9–10 (spring–fall 1979).

Yeah, I think that's right. And I don't even think they're creative. I don't think they have a place in the creative act. That is unless they're internalized.

I mean, after all, you choose to write some things and not other things—and you modify what you write. You're doing that kind of assessing all the time, but you're doing it. That's what being an artist *is*. And if you come in saying, "Here's something of mine. Is it any good?"—that's the kind of question that can't and shouldn't be answered.

That's a nonoperative kind of deal. I mean there's no profit on either side, it seems to me, in entering into that kind of question with a person who's trying to write. I know people do it all the time but it's just a thing that I try to avoid.

So the danger, then, as you see it, is that students will come to depend on a judgment of good or bad or right or wrong and for someone else to make that judgment rather than paying attention to the writer they are becoming . . .

Yeah, their own feelings.

. . . but being patted on the back.

Oh, yeah. That's another part, you know. It's like learning how to run by being given a milkshake every time you round the track. You soon dead-end in that kind of process.

Then where does *criticism come in as a process that can help students?*

Well, when a student comes to me with his poems and wants to know about them. I feel like a doctor with a patient. In order to diagnose anything, I have to ask first, "Where does it hurt?" Then whatever move *they* make allows a more human reaction and, if that student is unaware of any "hurt" or "pain" in their writing, then either the poems are OK or they're not really ready to see what it is that I might see. That is, if he's ready in his process of becoming a writer, he knows where it hurts. Even if it's so much as being able to say, "I can't put my finger on it but there's something wrong with this ending," then I might be able to help. But if a student is unaware of where his poem may be taking him—or going without him—why "hit" him? When he's ready to see it, he'll be ready to really see it, to understand it rather than just accept it because a teacher said such and such.

But it's more than that. Entering into this process has its own rewards whether or not your poetry goes somewhere. A teacher's job is not to be an assessor. That's the job of an editor. A student's work should be tracked, not corrected. And, if a dialogue develops that leads to better things, wonderful! But it must come from the student.

The problem sounds like it might be the competitive nature of our whole society.

That's right. And it's got nothing to do with poetry. I write down the center of my life. I've got to change my life to change my writing and I don't want to do that.

One of the things you said the other day was that art requires acceptance, that it requires an interchange that shows understanding and yet allows itself to occur freely. I'd like to translate that into a large question concerning the role and purpose of poetry in our lives. Should we focus on the craft of great poetry or should we encourage people to write it even if it's bad?

I think we should. I think we should encourage ourselves and others to write, to get into action, to play, to do all sorts of things—you know, music . . . everything! But, since we're on the one "R" of writing—anything that gets in the way of your feeling that it is possible to write and anything that gets in the way of your actually practicing writing or doing writing, it seems to me, is blocking the most important learning element that there is in it all—and that is performance, just doing it.

And so, I start out with this principle of removing obstacles to writing. And one of those obstacles that I find in class is that inhibition, that fear that what I do won't be so good. I say, "Forget it. Don't worry about it." And it is possible in class to get students to feel relaxed, I find.

For one thing, they're sort of jolted when I won't give critical reactions. I know it's a hazard but actually in class the students that I've met accommodated to it very well. They write like mad. They write *more* than they used to write.

. . .

Where does your idea of "no praise, no blame" come into play? Could you discuss that more fully?

Sure, and I think it relates to what we were just saying. There are people who try to induce students to get involved in literature and writing by giving them praise, the pat on the head, the competitive idea that "now you're getting ahead of so-and-so," and it's substituting a superficial gratification for the great sweep of gratification—that *real* involvement in art. That's one way to go at this idea of "no praise, no blame."

The other way is found in my desire to inhabit a world—and I want to inhabit a family and a circle of friends and a classroom— in which it's possible for us to give reactions forth, freely. Where, you know, you think of something, you say it. You don't double-check it with the government or with a teacher or with a parent who might be too hoverly or too oppressive. It's just a feeling of freedom. Blame would certainly operate to suppress that.

And I think that praise, in a more disguised way—but just as coercive—is also inhibiting. It makes you double-check any-thing that you are going to do because you're trying to find out whether you can get praise out of it. Whereas you should be saying it or writing it in terms of the satisfaction you feel, some-thing you've discovered. And, oh, I crave being in a world in which someone has an idea and they'll just tell me what the idea is instead of trying to figure out whether I've already had it and would like to hear someone else say it.

But have the public schools so fastidiously dealt with praise and blame and grades that to jump outside that system would be such a leap outside of student expectations that it might confuse them and might result in things you had not intended as a teacher? Can't you hear people saying that the students *aren't ready for this?*

[Laughs] Many people do tell me this, as a matter of fact. My own experience, though, is that students are ready, and, you know, it's a relief for them to be in a room in which they don't have to go through this, this game to change the gusto one can naturally feel for activities. For the kind of thing in which you have to make the rewards be outside the activity all the time is stultifying.

Actually, I think a lot of what I'm saying has been in the schools for a long time. John Dewey, for example, would be harmonious with this, though maybe what I should do is just settle down and say this: In my own experience, it's not been a hazard. Kids are ready for this kind of classroom. It's one of the startling things that happened to me. When I really tried it . . . all those fears . . . nothing! No problem.

Is all this related to an idea I heard you put forth, that art is inevitable— not good or bad? So that praise and blame should be divorced from the language of education, that they're not at all part of the process?

Sure it's related to that. We can all be in the arts. Sure we can. But I'd bring it locally—our workshop group here at Port Townsend. It's not that we don't appreciate each other, but people even joke now saying, "Hey, be careful not to praise me." Fundamentally, it means that you're accepting people and what they're doing. I want to be very careful not to say that "no praise, no blame" means coldness. I think it means warmth. It means, "Why, of course it's all right. It's all right even if it isn't all right."

So that the process shouldn't divorce a teacher from a student's work but, instead, be based on a realization that art requires or needs acceptance and an interchange that shows understanding?

I think that's right. If a student asks me if I understand what they've done, I'm ready. To what degree I understand it . . . well, we work it out.

I was thinking about no role playing. Where I come from the role playing in the classroom is usually that role that offers lollipops to people whose work you don't feel all that good about in order to encourage them to go on, or it is pretending that you can't understand their work because it is written on two sides of the paper or something like that. I'd rather come on the level. If I can understand it . . . yeah, I can understand it. Have I seen better work? Yeah, I've seen better work. Have I seen worse? Yeah.

You know, we've got to settle for where we are. When I write I don't expect to . . . be . . . I forgive myself. I'd like to forgive others.

It's quite clear that you've made a very clear distinction in your own life between education as imparting information and education as "educe-ing."

Yes, educing. I like that. Edu-cation, that calling forth, that leading forth of whatever comes from within.

Action—that's the word!

So is your advice to create, as much as possible, an atmosphere of open receptivity and encouragement?

Encouragement on *entering* the activity.

After that?

After that, you've got to begin to negotiate.

People who run learn how to run. People who swim learn how to swim. People who write learn how to write. And people change, at least I'd hope a class could change.

In our workshop, for instance, among the group of us, we sort of sense when someone is ready for the next thing we're ready to give them or whether someone needs to be lived with awhile before we do all those things that we might have done to somebody else's poem. I think that's the sort of general consensus feeling I'm in favor of. It just delays that important kind of growing up.

So, if it's organic criticism, it's OK, but, if it comes from outside as a standard, it's not?

Yeah. Now if I were a little more careful about the way I phrased this whole thing, maybe I wouldn't get myself into so much trouble with my writer-friends. I'll try to remember that.

Well, how would you rephrase this issue?

Well, I wouldn't say "no praise, no blame" in a talk unless I was trying to start an argument—which I was. Instead, I would sort of creep up on this issue about whether what we want from others is their advice about what to change, whether we want from others approval of what we're doing, whether we want them to be sure to warn us if we're doing the wrong thing. Wait. I know how to get at this a better way.

It worked out in one school where I was. I met the class the first day and it occurred to me to ask them, to put it to them like this:

"If you had your choice and you could have someone here teaching creative writing who could offer you either of these two things, which would you like? One would come in who was undoubtedly a very good writer and a sharp critic—perhaps the ranking poet of the country—and this poet would read your work and *tell* you where it goes wrong and could make your poems better and better towards publication and you would learn what's being sold and what editors want here and there and you would be published all over the country. You could have that or you could have someone in here who would meet you and look at your poems and help find out what kind of a person is writing these poems—the life that's in these poems, where is it going? How can this student get better and better in the center of the life that is them and develop forward into what is their unique place? In other words, instead of adapting for the market, get into the center of your life and write it."

They voted for the second.

And I'm not saying that the second wouldn't or couldn't bring about publication or the first the other way around—but I think it makes a difference how you phrase this and how you think about it when you go into the classroom.

So that the question challenges one's ultimate purpose: Is it to publish or is it to be a poet?

Yeah, and it sure, for me, is not getting published. It's something else. I mean I think that publication has to come incidentally.

Is there some connection between that idea and your own life as a writer that is simple and clear?

Yes, there is and I think it is simple and clear. I live in horror of becoming that kind of writer who is drafted into writing poems at the behest of an editor who's guiding my hands about what to write or of a leader of a literary school or a czar or a president. Instead, I thought the glory of freedom is—and it's much more important than political freedom—to find your own best life for yourself inside yourself.

And it's entering that process that does the civilizing. Stanley Kunitz has a very strong sense of an individual life finding its way by the radar it has inside it and I'd certainly harmonize with that.

I'd like to separate poems from poetry. You may learn how to do poems in any certain culture, whatever's current, whatever's stylish, whatever the editors want. But the best poems and all the significant poetry, it seems to me, come from this sort of thing we've been talking about—finding the center of your life, some kind of harmony between the self that's emerging with the unfolding of time and the language that's available right at that stage.

I think that individual poems are expendable but that trajectory of your life—that's the thing. The language is there, available to sustain you into new things . . . not to find your way back into things that someone else has found and wants to urge you to do again. It's much more adventurous than that! Poetry is right there at the edge where your life is interacting with the materials of your experiences. It's the difference between crafting individual poems and achieving the kind of concurrence and concordance with yourself from which the best and the original and the larger-than-civilization poems come.

Isn't that a superhuman task for teachers? Doesn't it demand too much that's so tentative and adroit?

It sounds scary but there are some fail-safe things in it. I think that freedom and encouragement both serve this process of poetry and it is fairly easy to find your way as a human being by means of your sympathies and feelings into that kind of relation with another human being that will induce and encourage freedom and sympathy and creativity.

So, yes, it's awesome and it's scary but it's also the thing that's the most native of all human talents. And, if we don't turn our backs on those processes that daily life keeps encouraging us to live by—like generosity . . . honesty . . . alertness . . . finding out what other people have to give us . . . a kind of openness to experience—*then* we'll find our way into the best poetry.

As a teacher, I trust those things. I mean I feel that I'm backed by all the major values of our culture. So, those things that are slogan words to come on the Fourth of July, to me turn out to be, when accepted, simply and gratefully, the very basis of the educational system. I'm not afraid of lining myself up with the positive elements of our society which I think all, when seen generously and clearly, are conducive to the life of poetry.

Given education as it now exists in America, are there any more specific pieces of advice that you could share with teachers which might be practical translations of these large values we've been discussing?

First I want to step back just a little bit. Part of the context in which you put this invites me to assess current schools.

Of the teachers I know many of them are doing a heroic job. I don't feel at all pessimistic about what the schools are doing. Or the teachers. My friends the teachers are right in there pitching. So, I have a lot of hope about that.

The advice I would give is: have the commitment and faith that's implied by the best parts of your life.

You have friends; treat the students as friends. You find it most advantageous to deal with people who honor their commitments, who are honest, who are sympathetic and open. Those values which many people say are absent from our lives *I* think are present in our lives.

So, just take a stand with sympathy, listening, responding. All those virtues that we have in each other as friends, it seems to me, are the basis for the best way to go into a classroom.

It's always encouraging to hear someone say for us those things we believe in but somehow forget from day to day. Is there any warning that might be worth remembering?

What comes to mind is Ambrose Bierce's *Devil's Dictionary* definition of a lad. It says, "A lad is a boy with a man's hand on his head." And I'd say avoid that. That kind of patronizing relationship.

Instead, enter into the full social relations with the class in terms of human beings. Don't demean them by saying "All the kids are dumb today" and things like that. I don't believe it anyway.

So, just be on the level. I think that would help quite a lot.

How about the students? Is there anything you can advise people who might want to be writers?

[Laughs] Keep on writing. Yeah. Write! Writers are persons who write!

Interviewing Tracker Dog

*A Fantasy before the Daily Craft Lecture
at Any Writers' Conference*

Tracker Dog, Tracker Dog, what are your plans
for finding the little child lost in the mountains?

Sniff-sniff, Sniff-sniff, Sniff-sniff

Tracker Dog, you are not answering my question.
I suspect you of being a romantic,
some kind of modern ignoramus.
Maybe you haven't even studied the tradition
that worthy tracker dogs before you have established.

Sniff-sniff, Sniff-sniff, Sniff-sniff

Now wait—surely you see the advantage
of outlining your objectives, of a rational approach.

Sniff-sniff, Sniff-sniff, Sniff-sniff

You ungrateful tracker dog, pretending
you never studied T. S. Beagle, or W. B.
Setter, or learned the trochaic lope
in order to have a foundation for running.

Sniff-sniff, Sniff-sniff, Sniff-sniff

All right, Tracker Dog—you'll never learn
the elegant line, the turns that make
a trail that we can admire and study.
You're not a worthy model for us.

Sniff-sniff, Sniff-sniff, Sniff-sniff

Unpublished, ca. 1988.

Waking Up in Bremerton

An Invocation

A couple of years ago, at Whitworth College, Patrick Todd said something that stays with me. He said, "When I write I enter a place where I have not been, and *sometimes* when I write I enter a place where I have longed to be."

How can we help each other today to achieve that readiness with language that will enable the approach to where we long to be? Maybe we can help each other find, in each of our lives, what is obscure but ready to be significant. I have brought a picture—I'll hold it up, but you don't have to see the details. It is of a track of a bear going out into the forest; you see the paw prints clearly, but you don't see until a second look that in the brush right in front of you is the bear itself, staring right into your eyes. How can we perceive what is ready for its effect? How can we stay alert enough?

I think that in a conference like this we need to transfer our attention from what an editor wants to what we have to give. You can't help being original, but if you learn to be original, what do you possess of the self you so abundantly represent? It's our individual reactions that count. Can we cling to that idea through this day?

This morning at breakfast David Hecker began to talk about his home state. He was talking along, and I noticed some words: "going from Wolf Point to Grand Forks by way of Waweekan," or something like that. And I thought, "How rich we are!" The language is always offering us bonuses. If we can just let the

---

From a talk delivered at the Writer's Workshop, June 1982.

emergences while we write have their influence, we can ride the surf. We can get somewhere we have always wanted to be.

So—trying to let the day guide me, I began to write this morning about things right around us. The birds were cranking up; I remembered seeing the battleships in the harbor; I began to feel how it is to be on an island. And I Wrote "Waking Up in Bremerton":

> Maybe this is the day the unfelt earthquake
> touches our island. Battleships asleep at their berth
> continue to dream the doom in their guns;
> the captains look at each other: "I didn't feel
> anything." "I didn't either." "It's all the same."
> But the unfelt earthquake has happened anyway.
>
> The world didn't know it. No one, captain or not,
> will notice; even the birds chirp on, announcing
> the same old miracle washing our shore again.
> But this island we're on floats in a new sea;
> the doom in the guns won't ever be the same.
> Strange things do happen. Maybe this is the day.

It matters little whether my morning writing ever becomes a piece that finds its way into publication, but to me it matters a lot that my daily practice has grown right out of immediate experience: being on an island (you may be used to this, but for some of us it feels different), remembering those battleships nuzzled up to the dock, wondering about "the doom in their guns"—a phrase that many of us can all too easily understand—even getting the birds outside my window into my day's writing. I feel secure in my writing, not either successful or unsuccessful, not correct or incorrect, just OK about it; for it is growing directly out of my situation, my current feelings, my natural talk.

If my plea for letting the day guide us seems too comfortable to you, let me speak savagely against the other way of approaching a workshop, against the "success-oriented" way. Here in my hand is a flyer I picked up in the library on campus. It is headed "How to Write with Style." It is a product of the advertising department of International Paper Company, which tells me at the end, "We believe in the power of the printed word." How gratifying.

The "how to write" essay on this page is by Kurt Vonnegut, a person I've met and enjoyed, for his wit, his readiness. But his contribution to International Paper Company's advertised belief in the power of the printed word gives me a drowning feeling. I am advised to consult Strunk and White in order to learn style. And in a wandering paragraph Kurt Vonnegut has this discouraging passage: "Lucky indeed is the writer who has grown up in Ireland, for the English spoken there is so amusing and musical. I myself grew up in Indianapolis, where common speech sounds like a band saw cutting galvanized tin and employs a vocabulary as unornamental as a monkey wrench."

These similes, these tap-dancing performances, tell me the presence of someone who, alas, has learned how to write. This page is not serious enough. We surely can find our way into areas of consideration more central to our lives than the elements of style or the figures of speech that will sell your product.

Somehow, the language that comes to you when you are truly available to immediate experience can bring you surprises, can enrich experience, can reveal profound connections between the self and the exciting wilderness of emerging time. I hope that we can help each other here today be alert for the bonuses that other people's writing experiences can give us. Our opportunity today relates to more than style, more than publication— it relates to integrity, the security of being in touch with what really has meaning within the self each of us happens to be.

Our Workshop Last Summer

At our workshop last summer we didn't make any mistakes.

Well, we did make a few adjustments, true, as we went along. But that's what a workshop is—you take what you have and make something useful of it.

What we took was—anyone. For anyone can make writing a way of life, a practice that can lead to self-realization, to a fuller involvement in one's own experience. And we were committed to help "transform everyday names, stories, dreams, and observation of life into poetry and lyrical prose."

Already, even that description marks ours as a certain kind of workshop. In many classes only certain writers are admitted, and their work is groomed for publication; their practice is guided toward the producing of pieces that will fit the market. You can choose that kind of instruction, and in fact for most people the general idea is to come for study so as to be able to break into print.

We didn't preclude publication as an aim, but ours was a different slant; we wanted to invite everyone into the enrichment that writing can offer. We wanted to escape that funneling effect of writing as imitation of the writing of others. No matter how you guard against teaching "the workshop poem" or "workshop story," just having a group intent on competition, on learning fast from each other and from literature, will enforce imitativeness. We wanted to help each other feel that whole tide of language jumping and swirling around us. We sought the feeling that comes for an innocent reader encountering a story or

---

From *The Writer,* April 1989.

poem, or for an innocent writer pursuing the process of discovery that creative writing is.

Our sessions were to achieve this gusto, this welcoming feeling that enables you to test your actions by the feelings you actually have, not the feelings you have been taught you should have, or the faked interest that comes from having a goal outside the process itself.

How can you get that?

You can pay a lot of attention to each other's writings, and we did that. We had formal sessions, the usual kind, in which copies of our work were passed around and discussed. But we carefully—even stealthily—wove in some differences.

In the very first session we passed around the following list of considerations for getting the most out of our meetings:

1. Please write notes on copies of the works we discuss; you can give your notes to the writer and in turn receive many responses to your work. No need to be definitive—any reactions may help.
2. What kind of notes would you like to receive? Be helpful in regard to the text in hand, but also note other opportunities suggested by the text before us.
3. Are there portable principles you come upon in our interchanges? Can you help us all recognize and retain and carry away from our conferences any ideas that may be lastingly helpful?
4. Be alert for hints in the texts that might carry over into new projects: "corrections" may be in order, but glimmerings of further possibilities are also to be sought.
5. Remember that the speaker in the poem or story is a created being. The writer is making something and should not be simply identified with the character speaking.
6. Are you submitting your best work? Your most troubled attempts? Your most representative?
7. What you take away from a workshop depends largely on the other people present and on the discussion of their works: how can we induce maximum help from the spread of talents among us?
8. Consider carefully: are we trying to correct writings before us

so that they will be the best possible pieces? the most likely to achieve publication? the least vulnerable to criticism? Or are we trying for something else?

Of course, that last one, "trying for something else," is the crucial nudge, the one most important to me for the rest of our week together. But other hints in that list also creep toward inducing the atmosphere needed in a workshop. For instance, all through the phrasing is the idea that everyone can help, and that anyone may be blundering into selfish or thoughtless assumptions about goals for our sessions.

As we went on through the first day, many additional *social* moves were elicited to give us momentum for our kind of workshop.

We found a big, plain wall like a bulletin board for our use, and we started the posting of current writings: anyone could put up for view a note, a finished work, an idea for the group. We encouraged each other to write messages on each other's work. The wall filled up; by the end of the week we were spilling around a corner, and we had achieved instant publication of the first stirrings of many poems and stories. Small as this move may seem, remember that those pieces on the wall probably achieved more readership—and more alert and informed readership—than do similar pieces in many literary periodicals. It was exciting.

And we found a table and a corner in a room where we could bring our own copies of literary material and make it handy reading for everyone. The need many at a workshop feel, to learn about publications that will help guide writers, or give writers places for seeking their work in print, was immediately met. The "library" came to be a meeting place for exchanging lore about editors and outlets. We could have had a better library; we should have asked in preliminary correspondence for such materials. That was a mistake, come to think of it, that we could not overcome quickly by adjustments at our conference. Next time . . .

We staggered our sessions through the day, so that "instructors" could visit around; everyone could pick and choose what to attend. This didn't work too well, for all the sessions got large; so we established a certain in-group of manageable size for each session and allowed auditors to sit outside the circle and listen. And in the spirit of the place, even those outside the circle, if moved irresistibly, could put in a word. This easiness of access was popular, and it worked out all right. If some point came up and got passed by, it could be discussed around in the swirl afterward.

One period of an hour or more in midafternoon we saved for a general meeting, where a leader could give a lecture on some factor or aspect of writing or publishing. Or such a period could be given over to readings by participants; from reluctance at first to a crowding of the schedule toward the end this kind of session came to flourish. It gave motivations, and it enhanced acquaintance, and it helped us all perceive the immediacy of writing and sharing.

When the demand for individual conferences began to crowd us, we improvised. We permitted—even invited—others to sit in on such conferences. The person who was the center of attention was not slighted, but a group could experience what came out of such focus on one person's work, and actual feedback, during the session, and after the session, was increased. If anyone required just the one-on-one encounter with an instructor, we adjusted to that, but most came to value the presence, the enrichment, of others.

A new kind of writing emerged—the self-review. Take something you have written, throw yourself into the critic's or the reviewer's stance, and analyze. Make your review into a creative work in itself. The wall began to blossom in these reviews; people, once they got invited to stand back from their own work, could achieve perspective and surprise themselves with insights. And of course there was room for playfulness and irony. No one else can be so insightful and authoritative as you can about the being who produced your work.

Other moves came along as we treated our workshop as an occasion for taking what we had and making best use of it. One such development was that we used the talents of a teacher of dance, who held a half-hour session at the beginning of each day for anyone who cared to come—"improvisational warm-up for mind and body." These gatherings of a dozen or so fervent believers sometimes were treated to live music by a neighboring flute workshop, and a feeling of serendipity prevailed when we could cock our ears to the more distant workshop on the tuning of the steel drum. . . .

It didn't hurt us any that we had other resources for our improvisations—a resort town down the street, a beach right beside us for campfires, for walks, for materials to weave into our writings. But what really counted was whether during the week the people involved gained in their gusto for writing and gained in the degree to which their own lives became more discovered, more touched into involvement with the flexibility and imagery and strengthening that language can give.

.　.　.

We felt lucky as we closed down our workshop. We ended with a group picture, a passing out of our anthology of productions in the week together, and a resolve to keep writing, stay in touch, and meet at a workshop again.

Workshop Gleanings

19 Oct 1987

Is it possible to identify some central quality or distinctive essence in each poem?

Could it be that each of us is pursuing an individual course in our writing that could make a contribution to the realizations of all others?

And is each of us blindly neglecting possible ways to go that our habits or limitations have prevented our becoming aware of?

Are we in the habit of relying on limited senses—sight, for instance—in most of our writing?

How can we induce and preserve in ourselves the zest, the appetite, that sustains this value we sense in the life of writing?

21 Oct 1987

If you discern that your writings reveal chauvinism, prejudice, or whatever, should you change them? Should you change yourself? Will changing such writings change you?

Could some kind of allegiance—religion, country, race, political stance, love—enhance your writing?

Unpublished, October 19–23, 1987.

Is a writing workshop for cultivating a skill? Is that skill connected to character?

We say a word has meaning—does a construction have meaning? Does a changed word-order change a meaning? Does leaving out punctuation have meaning? Does alluding by means of a full predication have a different meaning than alluding by means of a dependent element?

What a poem starts out being it keeps on being.

23 Oct 1987

Can you learn how to do poems that demonstrate skill but lack heart?

Is there value in doing (participating in) poetry that transcends profit, success, social value?

Today there's a hollow place where scripture was, where ritual was, where the story of our lives was. Language wanders back and forth there, lost, reaching for echoes that it finds, or makes. . . .

Grooming a Poem after It Happens

Put your writing under a good light. Turn your brights on and look at it.

Does the reader find early and sustained rewards?

Is the beginning just fixing to commence to begin? Can you take out some of that scaffolding you felt you needed when you were writing it?

Is there a part of your poem that might be moved to the beginning to enhance the effect? And if you moved that alive part to the beginning, could you then find a way to bring other parts of the poem up to the promise of the start?

How about the line breaks? Are there enticing beginnings to the lines? And hovering possibilities at the ends of lines? Can the reader be carried along better, or teased into leaning forward at places, instead of just being allowed to sit back and wait for some kind of *later* rewards?

Test the language of the poem. Is it evident in places that you are soliciting an indulgent reader to accord your poem credit just because it touches on already-achieved "poetic" elements? Are you coasting along on fads or cheap identifications with the lazy expectations of the reader? Or can you juggle the language a little and shake up the reader?

Unpublished, n.d.

Are there places where the sound, the cadence, the congruence between sound and meaning could become more helpful? If you changed order or stanza breaks could you be more dramatic?

Could your poem be revised *outward*, be the start of something you have just glimpsed and then not developed?

Could your poem be revised *inward*, dropped back on itself (for instance, at the end) to live by its stronger elements and not doilied up for the admiration of readers who like merely to nod their recognitions?

Have you given an editor or other reader occasion to wake up and call out, "Hey! Take a look at this"?

Five Writing Exercises

1. Tracking Yourself into a Poem

Poems are waiting to happen all the time. One way to encourage the happening is just to start with anything—any word or syllable, any feeling or thought, any formulation, cliché, noble or ignoble stance—and let the beginning have its own freedom to link forward through interaction with your self. Allow the chances, emergencies (emergences) to scatter forward on the page. That forwarding will find its pattern, from you, from your circumstances, from the *now* part of your life. What occurs to you deserves at least your temporary indulgence; from that indulgence (in words) will come further discovery.

For an exercise in such onwarding, try writing about any scene or journey. Rely on actuality all you like, but let the language begin to guide you—even mistakes as you make them could become bonuses: learn to relax into the feel of what is happening to you as you drift into the unfolding of what you are saying.

Here are some nudges toward such writing—not assignments or requirements, but just some possible ways to go:

> Think of something that happened when you were younger— what occurs to you will occur for some reason. Let that reason take over the way you remember and the part of the experience you begin to set down. If your impulses carry you into distortions of the actual experience, indulge those impulses—let the memory become the way it wants to become, and the way the language begins to suggest that it become.
>
> Or imagine a journey: begin your way into your house or your town—or into what you wish was your house or your town.

Let the language of your report on this journey become like a dream—allow the journey to reveal itself and to sequence along in the mode of psychological appropriateness—let the scenes be satisfying to the self you are.

Be brave. Make mistakes. Don't try to make "a good poem"— just blunder into the discoveries that come from action.

2. An Elementary Exercise

A teacher assigned an elementary exercise: draw a map, a layout of someplace where you have lived; list four things—just objects—in each room or in each corner of the yard, or around each section of the neighborhood. After you have listed these objects, tease out of your recollections some account that uses references to what you have listed. Forcing myself to tractor childishly along, I quickly sketched a place, a house where we used to live, and listed objects. After doing that we were to write an account, for a special reason. I mean a very special reason. We had to wait till we had those objects. In the arts, *things* make a difference. And touching things makes literature. I recall the story of the Greek hero whose mother was the earth. As he journeyed, he met many of those brutal champions that used to travel around in those days. They would contend with him and throw him to the ground, but every time he touched the earth, he got up stronger. He was finally killed by Hercules, who held him above the earth and strangled him to death. Well, writers too need to touch the earth; it is a source of strength to them. So were these objects I listed in the exercise. Here is the account that grew out of that list:

108 East Nineteenth

Mother, the sweet peas have gushed out of
the ground where you fell, where you lay that day
when the doctor came, while your wash kept flapping
on the line across the backyard. I stood
and looked out a long time toward the Fairgrounds.
The Victrola in the living room used to play

"Nola," and the room spun toward a center
that our neighborhood clustered around. Nasturtiums
you put in our salad would brighten our tummies,
you said, and we careened off like trains
to play tag in alfalfa fields till the moon
came out and you called us home with "Popcorn
for all who come." But that was long
before you said, "Jesus is calling me home."

And Father, when your summons came you quietly
left, no one could hold you
back. You didn't need to talk
because your acts for years had already prayed.
For you both, may God guide my hand in its pious
act, from far off, across this page.

The process of recalling, touching, being yoked into assignments, forced me to load what I wrote with particulars. The Victrola for instance—actually as I remember, it was a wind-up machine called a Brunswick. But in my poem—writers lie a little—it became a Victrola. I especially needed to call it that because what occurred to me for it to play was "Nola." Now about the fairgrounds. We lived near the Kansas State Fairgrounds. I hadn't realized what it means to live near the fairgrounds—the *fair* grounds—until my poem. What I am trying to emphasize here is that getting into the process reinforced my life. I had lived by the fairgrounds, and the fairgrounds was not a live metaphor for me at the time; it was just a place where we played. But in my poem I realized that the fairgrounds, and the nasturtiums, and the alfalfa, and the popcorn, were all important to me. Through these particulars, my activity carried me with accelerating excitement toward realizations I would not have had if my writing had not carried me there.

·   ·   ·

3. Robert Bly's Working-with-Things Project

The following piece of writing came about at a recent "Great Mother" conference at Little Lake Elkhart, in Wisconsin. This is the way I noted the circumstances of our writing project at the time:

In the afternoon Robert Bly leads about fifteen of us down by the lake for one of his "thing" poems exercises. He tells us to go down to the lake and each one to pick up three wet objects to bring back. We do, and he says to choose one of them—"You'll know which one when you look them over." After that he leads us through a succession of writing exercises, each one to be complete before he tells us the next to do, e.g.: "Describe the object. Did you tell how heavy it is?" "Now tell how it feels to your hand." "Now what is inside it, what it is like?" "What shape is it?" "Now compare it to your mother." (This last one shakes us all loose from our plodding ways.) "Now compare it to the princess who sewed shirts to save her six brothers." (A reference to a folktale we had all listened to during the conference.)

I finished a prose description, along with the required comparisons, about a handful of mud with a muskrat print on it that I had scooped up at the lakeshore. . . .

Find three wet things on the shore; then describe one—size, feel, smell, shape.

Whiskers of roots brush out from this wet, swarthy glob of mud. It is only a frog-sized piece of the earth—cool and damp, it feels alive almost, or at least ready to be alive if urged by the fingers. It might jump and leave you for its place where you found it.

What right did you have to scoop it away just because a track on this fistful of mud caught your attention? The muskrat that first felt it last night just went on shaking its foot maybe and wondering whether its track would be taken for art, one toe so elegantly splashing a signature separately and as if considering it might become a thumb sometime, should other nights invite a foot-loose rat for a stroll.

But mud has designs of its own, inside, where pieces of moss have squirmed their own patterns, where a sliver of charcoal dives through old leaves. The smell of the lake lives here, and a faint residue from loon sounds that sank at night and stayed still, hidden from the ice fingers that scrabbled for light.

Now relate it to your mother.

My mother, soft as mud, couldn't survive if we left. She clung with tendrils as fragile as these fragments of root. When she lifted me, my hands imprinted her yielding face as we nuzzled into those last warm days of summer.

Now I have found this mud, understanding on the cluttered shore, except that the track of a muskrat, or my track left over for years, left a print that now reaches my face through the dry air, here, safe but far.

Now relate it to the princess who sewed star shirts to save her six brothers.

Could a princess that steadfastly remained silent to save her swan brothers be more quiet and true than this unnoticed fragment abiding through centuries on the shore? Now the madness of sound—motorboats, loud cars, clashing oars—arches into this day, but the handful of mud has joined my hand to her hand, and the coldness of the deep water is mine, even in the sun.

I have kept silence and woven a star-flower coat for my mother, through the help of a friend who guided me back through tunnels and roots to the dark charcoal hidden too well to be found by the wise or learned or strong.

4. Multiple Poems from One First Draft

A couple of summers ago sponsors of a writers' workshop at the University of Wyoming asked me to send ahead some notes along with successive revisions that led to a poem completed and ready for publication.

I did that, and in the shuffle of papers one workshop participant got my first notes and assumed that the job was for students to make a poem from them. When I showed up and did my act, talking about my successive drafts and the final poem, the student came forward and showed me the poem that grew from my notes when he considered them. To my surprise, he had veered a great deal from the direction I thought my notes indicated they should go.

On considering, I saw that even I could lean a certain way and achieve other poems, based on the original notes. All I did was start all over again for one poem further from the notes, but this incident set me to thinking—maybe one could do a whole book from the doodling that seemed at the time to be starting toward only one end. . . .

My own first poem from the notes has just been accepted by *Poetry*. I have the other poem in circulation. If all goes well, maybe I'll make a career out of reincarnating those enigmatic notes.

5. Last Day's Assignment

See Something

Full length, a grassblade saws a stone.

"Tracking Yourself into a Poem," unpublished, n.d. "An Elementary Exercise," from "When Writers Get Together," *Literature and Belief,* 1982; "108 East Nineteenth," from *An Oregon Message* (New York: Harper and Row, 1987); "Robert Bly's Working-with-Things Project," from Thomas R. Smith, ed., *Walking Swiftly* (New York: Ally Press, 1992); "Multiple Poems from One First Draft," unpublished, n.d.; "Last Day's Assignment: *See Something,*" unpublished, August 1972.

Soul Food

We writers try to help each other, sometimes. But there is a catch in this generosity: if you begin to rely only on what others say about your work, you may become like a compass that listens to the hunches of the pilot. You may be good company, but you are useless as a compass—a writer, I mean.

So, when we meet, say at a conference or workshop, we look each other in the eye with an estimate hovering between us. We know that our kind of activity has some complexities not evident to others, and we wonder if those complexities will be recognized in any interchanges about our craft.

For instance, we know that our work is insufficiently judged if much time is given over to assessing the topics of our work. We know that a critic who discusses whether we talk enough about Nicaragua or not, or human rights or not, or the general topic of enlightenment or not, is missing the mark.

We know that there is something supremely important in the creating of a story or poem that all too often will escape the attention of an outsider trying to assess it. And for those outsiders, general readers, even critics, it may not be devastating if they talk at large: the main point is that such readers be affected, no matter what they ascribe our influence to. But for us writers it would be fatal to be misled by superficial assessments; and in fact one of the main hazards for a "successful" writer may be the insidious intrusion of those outer assessments on the inner process that allows us writers to find our way.

We must have an inner guide that allows us to rove forward throughout the most immediate impulses that come our way.

Unpublished, n.d.

For us, our whole lives are our research; and caught up by our best subjects we become not just an expert, but the only expert there is. We have to be the sole authority for what comes toward us, where we are, with our unique angle of seeing.

If the most significant writing comes from this inner guidance, who will help you find it? Would it be someone who interposes the considerations of the marketplace while the delicate time of discovery is going on? Would it be the person who puts primary emphasis on your imitation of forms and strategies?

Let me plead, not for ignoring advice from wherever it comes, but for allowing in your own life the freedom to pay attention to your feelings while finding your way through language. Besides that audience out there in the world, there is some kind of ideal audience that you have accumulated within your individual consciousness—within your conscience!—and abiding guidance is your compass, one that constitutes what you have to contribute to discourse with others.

Moving back and forth from the inner to the outer world (it feels good) might be the way to your best writing.

Into the unknown you must plunge, carrying your compass. It points at something more distant than any local guidance. You must make "mistakes"; that is, you must explore what has not been mapped out for you. Those mistakes come from somewhere; they are disguised reports from a country so real that no one has found it. When you study that country, shivers run down your back—what a wilderness out there! What splendid stories flicker among those shadows! You could wander forever.

Odd words keep occurring to you, pauses, side glances—mysterious signals. What hidden prejudice brought that next word into your mind? If you hastily retreat to an expected progression, what shadowy terrain might you be neglecting? What revelations might you miss by any "expert" weaving of another well-crafted poem or story?

Like Don Quixote on his unorthodox steed you must loosen the reins and go blundering into adventures that await any traveler in this multilevel world that we too often make familiar by our careful threading of its marked routes between accustomed places.

And like Don Quixote you must expect some disasters. You

must write your bad poems and stories; for to write carefully as you rove forward is to guarantee that you will not find the unknown, the risky, the surprising.

Art is an activity in which the actual feel of doing it must be your guide; hence the need for confidence, courage, independence. And hence the need for guardedness about learning too well the craft of doing it.

By following after money, publication, and recognition, you might risk what happened to the John Cheever character who in like manner "damaged, you might say, the ear's innermost chamber where we hear the heavy noise of the dragon's tail moving over the dead leaves."

Being Tough, Being Gentle

Chekhov has a story about an old cabbie who drives his horse all day—through miserable weather and with many passengers—always wanting to tell someone about what is nearest his heart. No one has time to listen, and at the end of the day while unhitching his horse the cabbie finally finds a listener: he tells his unbearable trouble to his horse.

Sometimes we writers must feel like that cabbie. We have to provide what editors want to publish, what readers want to read. We drive hard all day, ignoring what is so near our hearts that we don't know how to handle it. It's too private, too personal. Sometimes we can hardly face, even within our own selves, those significant feelings. But surely what my whole life most wants to say can motivate my writing. Surely I need not abandon what I value, just in order to be fashionable, or to meet some editor's whim. What kind of life—what kind of vocation—is that? So—how to be serious, emotional, have a real life—but not fall into sentimentality. How can we carry our most fervent feelings right into the living room of our readers and still be firm, solid, satisfying, convincing?

First, we can remember the usual warnings: "Show me, don't tell me." "Avoid clichés." "Get images and sense impressions into the lines." "Don't just say 'love,' 'beauty,' 'heart,' 'tears.' " "When you find yourself terribly fond of what you are saying, watch out!" "You can't do it with adjectives. . . ." We can observe these warnings. We can curry our writings by applying remedies. But somehow just observing such rules is not enough. They trim

From *The Writer,* May 1991.

away, but they don't supply the fire we need. And they don't invite us to cut loose with our whole sentient being.

Once a writing class met at a game reserve—Malheur—in eastern Oregon. The place seethed with birds, and miles of cattails, willows, wandering waterways, buttes where coyotes howled. When as teacher I drove out there, the class gathered at a picnic table, and we looked around. One of the students said, "This place is beautiful."

Another chimed in, "This is the most beautiful place I have ever seen."

The next one got even more creative: "Hey, I've never even dreamed of so beautiful a part of the world!"

And I said, "We have to get out of here."

Our senses were overloaded, and we were not able to lean back enough to muster evidence rather than incoherent cries.

Maybe that's it. Maybe we have to practice writing about topics that allow us some degree of balance, of emotional stability from whence we can lever into the language some evidence for what we are feeling. That's the safe way. But we don't want to be safe at the cost of shying from our most enticing subjects.

Here is how in a workshop recently one writer—Lou Crabtree—achieved control by putting her ultimate topic, "Burial," into the form of an Indian ceremony:

> In the morning
> they will bury you
> standing on the north side
> the south the west
> not one will stand
> no shadow will fall
> on the east side
> no evil spirit between
> you and the sunrise.

Another writer in the workshop headed bravely into that most difficult of "sentimental" topics, a poem about her dog. She avoided some booby traps by *denying* her feelings (you can't mention something without its having an effect; it will be pres-

ent, but it may be saved from being discounted by the reader).
She called her poem "Sorrow":

> The black dog by the road
> two days in a row can't be yours.
> He died nine years ago. It's been
> that long since you saw him last.
> The plumed curl of his tail as he left
> through woods and you holding
> the leash limp in your hands . . .

The elements of sentiment are present, but insulated by being
denied. Ruth Moose, the author of "Sorrow," was able to spell
out a touching experience but still be "tough."

These writers found ways to express honest feelings, and in
each instance they brought *additional* material into the text.
From their example, and from other such experiences, I want to
suggest that one way out of sentimentality is to allow—to em-
brace, even—more feeling, not less. We can be as honest and
fervent as our emotions suggest, and can explore those emo-
tions, write them out fully and warmly, adding the particulars
that identify exactly how the experiences come about. We can
tell the place, the people, the stray backgrounds that go to-
gether and create momentum—tell the reader exactly how it is,
not our summary of how we feel, but an elaboration of encoun-
ters that bloom into something new.

Don't try to impose your feelings on the reader by asserting
fervently *that* you have emotion, but instead, ask yourself *why*.
Was there a scene that accompanied your feelings? What time of
day was it? Does any sound relate to your feeling? There must
have been something that made you react, that makes you react
now. Make the reader encounter the human involvements that
command our emotions. The reader must face the evidence, not
just your soliciting of a feeling.

For—remember—literature and the writing of it do more
than just express the self: literature creates whole new continents
of experience. David Copperfield, for instance, is not just op-
pressed by a cruel parent—his deadly, hard new father appears

with a name: Murdstone. When that father oppresses him, David doesn't only feel bad; he gets shipped away into a whole succession of momentous encounters, where he doesn't just meet strange people—he meets exactly identified characters, like an old man named Mr. Dick who flies kites and frequently gets immobilized by thinking of King Charles's head. These examples remind us that writers don't just assert summary feelings: Emily Dickinson doesn't just recollect a death in the family—she hears a fly buzz, and Death in the form of a kindly hack driver picks her up and starts down a long—a never-ending—road.

Writing—literature—springs new experience into being; it is much more than just partially achieved recollections transferred from a fervent author to an accepting reader: a new life springs into focus, by being told. To create means to change, to change writer and reader.

I never came back to earth after reading Chekhov.

Now when I reach for my book—or my pen—Mr. Murdstone raises his heavy cane. I hear a fly buzz. Beyond the hedge in a gush of color and laughter Mr. Dick releases his gigantic, staggering kite to the wind.

What Is a Current Event?

More and more in literature class the students listen less and less to the books; the books are about something that has already happened, or that didn't happen at all. Whereas all good students know that real events, current events, important events are happening every day, outside there, away from literature. It is like a big bass drum beating outside the window. Who can study against that throb?

And yet, the trouble with those big events is that they happen to other people; how about the current events that happen to us—to you and me? Inside here, away from the bass drum, current events happen; and the drum cannot become loud enough to drown out the important events inside, the really current, really important, events.

This morning an army of a million men crossed the thirty-eighth parallel in Korea. That's a current event, but only in terms of the real little events that compose it. One soldier was walking along on the dusty road carrying a pack that was too heavy and that had a knob that dug into his back. He hadn't been able to eat breakfast; he was thinking about how the road ahead looked like the road out north of the home town. When he stopped to adjust his pack an enemy rifleman, a hungry, cold man lost from his group, raised his gun, sighted over the smudgy barrel, and shot the soldier. That is a current event.

At the time of the crossing a diplomat in a neutral country was drinking his coffee. He put down his napkin and answered the phone. Now he would have to hurry to the consulate, prepare a report, stop by to pick up the groceries, put out of his

---

Unpublished, after February 24, 1951.

mind the thought of helping his son with his schoolwork. The diplomat's coffee was cold when he put down the receiver. That's a current event.

In the house of the commanding general the room was cold. He had to leave the telephone to go call for more fuel; during his absence the phone rang for advice, but the reply was delayed; one sector of the front delayed too long; the wave of advance was over; hundreds of men died. And the general found the orderly, who found the oil for the stove, which heated the room. That is a current event.

In our room one student read the story for today and saw in it something that changed his life. That story, the reading of it, was a current event. The bass drum was beating outside.

The front line was stabilized again; the enemy commander had gone out for fuel too; his troops waited too long and a mountain pass filled with snow. The lines settled back to where they were before. Millions of people experienced millions of events, all of them current. The editor beat the drum for certain events; hearts beat for others. And the experiences that make events, they are where you find them—and most of them not in the sound of the drum.

How These Words Happened

In winter, in the dark hours, when others
were asleep, I found these words and put them
together by their appetites and respect for
each other. In stillness, they jostled. They traded
meanings while pretending to have only one.

Monstrous alliances never dreamed of before
began. Sometimes they last. Never again
do they separate in this world. They die
together. They have a fidelity that no
purpose or pretense can ever break.

And all of this happens like magic to the words
in those dark hours when others sleep.

From *Passwords* (New York: HarperPerennial, 1991).

UNDER DISCUSSION
David Lehman, General Editor
Donald Hall, Founding Editor

Volumes in the Under Discussion series collect reviews and essays about
individual poets. The series is concerned with contemporary American and
English poets about whom the consensus has not yet been formed and the
final vote has not been taken. Titles in the series include: